Designing the Obvious

A Common Sense Approach to Web Application Design

Designing the Obvious:
A Common Sense Approach to Web Application Design
Robert Hoekman, Jr.

New Riders
1249 Eighth Street
Berkeley, CA 94710
510/524-2178
800/283-9444
510/524-2221 (fax)

Find us on the Web at: www.newriders.com
To report errors, please send a note to errata@peachpit.com

New Riders is an imprint of Peachpit, a division of Pearson Education
Copyright © 2007 by Robert Hoekman, Jr.

Editor: Wendy Sharp
Production Editor: Hilal Sala
Copyeditor: Jacqueline K. Aaron
Proofreader: Amy Standen
Compositor: ICC Macmillan
Indexer: FireCrystal Communications
Cover design: Robert Hoekman, Jr.
Interior design: Joan Olson

ISBN 0-321-45345-X
9 8 7 6 5 4
Printed and bound in the United States of America

This book is dedicated to anyone who has ever used a Web application and resented the experience.

Contents

Acknowledgements

When I was 17 years old, I met the girl who eventually became my wife. Her name is Christine Rose Pearson. Without her, none of this means anything. To Christine: thank you for being my inspiration.

Of course, this book could never have been written without my editor, Wendy Sharp. Aside from knowing exactly how to get me to write the best book I possibly could, she was smart enough to know what needed to be edited, and wise enough to know what didn't. Wendy, you are a master of your craft, and I am very lucky to have been able to work with you.

To Seth Godin, Jason Fried, Ryan Carson, Josh Williams, and Abe Fettig: thank you for your wonderful contributions to this book, and for proving it's possible to design the obvious.

To my friend and partner at 33Inc, Kris Hadlock: thank you for being one of those rare developers who really understands the importance of a good user experience.

To Hilal Sala: thank you for making things run so smoothly during the production process and for your care and diligence.

To Nancy Davis: thank you for jumping in at the end, right when you were needed the most, to tie up all the loose ends and send this book out into the world.

To Jacqueline Aaron, my copy editor: your insight and skill have helped make this a great book. Thank you for your dedication, and for caring enough to speak up.

To Andreas Schueller and Mimi Heft: thank you for turning my rough design into the polished work of art that graces this book's cover. Without you, it wouldn't be nearly as good. To Amy Standen, thanks for your incredible attention to detail, and for providing the second, third and fourth set of eyes that we needed to proof everything.

To Joan Olson, the book's interior designer: you did a perfect job on this one. I couldn't be happier. Thanks for your incredible attention to detail.

Finally, to the authors and designers that have most inspired me to rise up and design the obvious: thank you to Hillman Curtis, Jesse James Garrett, Alan Cooper, Steve Krug, Donald Norman, and Seth Godin (again). You showed me the light, armed me with knowledge, and sent me on my way. Since then, I've had a few revelations of my own, but I couldn't have done it without you.

Author Biography

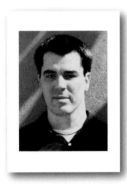

Robert Hoekman, Jr., is a professional Interaction Designer and Usability Specialist who has worked with GoDaddy.com, Macromedia, Adobe, United Airlines, Cisco Systems, and countless others to provide superior user experiences to a wide range of audiences.

In addition to his other writing credits, Robert authored the movie-based training course *Flash User Experience Best Practices,* the Flash design basics book *Flash Out of the Box,* and the seven-part InformIT.com series "Designing the Obvious."

Fantastic. I knew it was something simple like that.

1

Defining the Obvious

- ▶ What Is 'the Obvious'?
- ▶ How Do You Design the Obvious?
- ▶ The Framework for Obvious Design

Recently, while explaining over dinner what I do for a living, the people around me began relating horror stories about Web sites and software, complaining about the difficult experiences they have every single day with so-called productivity tools.

For one person, it was one of those new-fangled accounting packages that's supposed to make the job of managing client and employee records more cost-effective. For another, it was a library catalog. Hors d'oeuvres were passed around. Jokes were made. Drinks were refilled.

With each complaint, the voices grew louder. Everyone began speaking over each other, cutting each other off at every opportunity with new anecdotes.

Conversation turned into frustration. Friendly words turned into overwhelming disdain. Feathers were ruffled.

I nodded my head at the recounting of each awful experience. I understand their frustration. I've seen it myself. I hear the grumbling that results from constant exposure to difficult interactions. In fact, part of my job is to listen to these complaints and decide what to do with them.

When my recent dinner conversation calmed a bit, I tried to describe the typical design and development process and expounded a bit about it.

I explained that good Web-based software design is about understanding the principle activity your product is meant to support so you know what to build, and more importantly, what not to build. It comes from knowing the best ways to implement each feature so they make sense to the people using them. It comes from a deep understanding of the Web and how it works. It comes from knowing how people use computers, and having the ability to create something that works with users instead of against them. And I said great Web applications come from knowing what qualities make great Web-based software great.

I carried on for a little while. I tend to ramble when I think I'm saying something intelligent. But somewhere in there, I stumbled across a phrase that seemed to elicit a look of enlightenment on the faces of those listening. In a very Zen moment, I said:

"It's about designing the obvious."

And with that, agreement entered the dialogue. Frustration turned back into conversation. Overwhelming disdain turned back into friendly words. Feathers were unruffled.

Everyone agreed it would be lovely if I could do something about the particular products they lose arguments to on a daily basis. I can't, of course, because I have my own products to worry about, but I can do one thing.

I can tell you how to make *your* products better in hopes that someday Web developers and users will happily coexist, and communication between these fighting parties will be successfully bridged by the one thing they have in common: the interface.

See, the Web has exactly three layers.

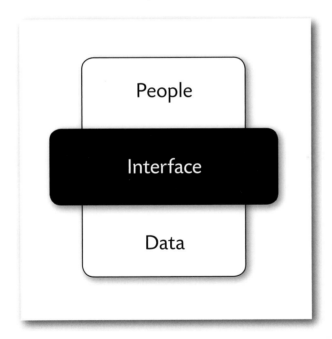

The Web world is divided into three layers: people, data, and the interfaces that stand between them.

The first layer is the **people layer**. There's nothing in this layer but people. People, people, and more people. People who have information, use information, and want more information.

The third layer is the **data layer** (I'll explain the second layer in a moment). Everything in the cyberworld that people need to know lives in the data layer: All the customer records, statistics, bookmarks, reference materials, finances, movie times, gas mileage, and popcorn cooking instructions live in the data layer.

The second layer is the one we deal with the most as Web developers. It's the **interface layer**. The applications used to connect people with data are in the interface layer. Everything from Flickr to Amazon, from Google to Basecamp. These applications manage data and present it to us. They let us play around with it, churn it up, spit it out, translate it, decipher it, encode it, and sleep on it. The only difference between these applications is what kind of data is used and what people do with it.

Interfaces stand between people and their data, providing access to the data like a door from one room to another. But no application I've ever seen is as simple to use as a door.

It's time that changed. And that's what this book is about.

That said, let's get on with it.

▶ What Is 'the Obvious'?

In addition to designing software, I also, as you might guess, *use* software. And I, like many people whether they realize it or not, tend to "hire" software the same way I would hire a person. I look for certain qualities, like a helpful nature, reliability, trustworthiness, and other things I'd expect to find in a good Boy Scout. Mostly, I look for the ability in a prospective employee (in this case, the software) to get work down in a smart and timely fashion so I can feel extra productive as a result of having hired the software. I look for characteristics that make me say, "Hey, you're swell. I'd like to work with you, take you under my wing, and invite you over for brunch. Come, join me in a game of Parcheesi."

Software, however, often interrupts me while I'm working, tells me I've made a mistake, refuses to help out in a useful way when I get stuck, spends a lot of time revealing things about how it works instead of simply telling me the job is done, and exhibits many other behaviors I find undesirable in employees. But usually I'm stuck with it. I can't find a way to live without the product because it's so valuable to my work, for whatever reason. I can't simply trade it in for something that may or may not be better, so I suffer through it. I yell at it, procrastinate dealing with it, and complain about it, but I live with it. This, of course, bugs me to no end.

These issues are not the result of an obvious design. An obvious design would let me get in, get what I need, and get out without spending any time at all thinking about how the software works or how to work with my data.

The goal of every Web-based software company should be to design applications that are so intuitive that the people using them attribute their ability to use them effectively to pure common sense. The design should make things clear. The products should be simple to understand, easy to learn, well organized. Interface elements should be intuitive, streamlined, uniform.

That's what makes an obvious design.

Software shouldn't force users to understand how it works so they can learn to do things with it. It shouldn't make them wonder if something has gone wrong and all their changes are about to be lost. It shouldn't spend a lot of time and effort interrupting their work to tell them something has broken and there's nothing they can do about it but click **OK**. It's *not* OK.

The people using our software every day want to get what they need and move on. Very often, they're not like us. We're geeks. Normal people don't sit in front of their computers all day because they enjoy it. They do it because they have to.

They put down their money and/or valuable time and make an investment in our Web applications. They have a reason for using the applications. They have goals. They have needs. They have expectations. And invariably, they have work to do.

We, the people who make the software, need to stop giving users excuses and start showing them results. We need to stop shoving modal error messages in their faces and start being polite. We need to stop talking down to them. Our users should be able to walk away from their computers feeling empowered. Productive. Respected. Smart.

Fortunately, this is all possible. And no, it's not nearly as complicated as you might think. We just need to start *designing the obvious*.

At this point in Web history, there are quite a few really great applications out there. Sure, they all have their own problems, but overall, many of them are swell. And we can learn from them. Backpack, Blinksale, DropSend, Google Page Creator, Blogger, and many others are all excellent examples of how Web applications can be made simple, effective, and most of all, *obvious*. Throughout this book, we'll look at the qualities that make applications like these so great, and discover how to create them in our own applications so our users can at last reach Web bliss.

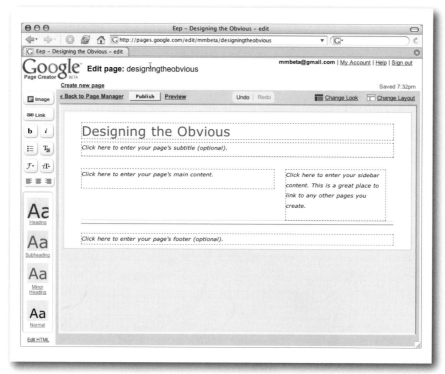

Google Page Creator makes it obvious how to perform the most common tasks when adding content to a Web page, such as formatting text and creating links.

Qualities of a great application

So what makes an application obvious?

When I sat down to write a list, it came very easily. I've used a lot of software, and much of it is now Web based. I've used everything from Web-based word processors to data dashboards, from calendaring applications to blogging tools, from site builders to room planners.

Over the years, I've paid attention to the qualities that make some products great and others miserable. I've stockpiled notes and documents and images and flowcharts and screen shots. Here's what I've seen. Your list may differ—and yes, I definitely encourage you to write your own, either from scratch or by expanding on this one.

Great Web-based software, in my experience, has some or all of the following qualities:

- It conforms to the way users interact with the Web, but focuses on the activity instead of a specific audience.

- It has only those features that are absolutely necessary for users to complete the activity the application is meant to support.

- It supports the user's mental model of what it does.

- It helps users get started quickly so they can become intermediate users as soon as possible.

- It makes it easy to recover from mistakes and difficult to make them in the first place.

- It has uniformly designed interface elements, but leverages irregularity to create meaning and importance.

- It reduces clutter to a minimum.

Each of these qualities has been documented as the result of studies in human-computer interaction, usability testing, and user-satisfaction surveys. The interesting part is that these qualities usually go unnoticed. Why? Because good software makes itself invisible. It enables users to do what they need to do and gets its behind-the-scenes operations out of the way so they can do it well. That's what makes it obvious.

The good news is that the items in the preceding list are not only noticeable, if you know what to look for, they are also reproducible.

Yes, indeedy. *You can design them.*

▶ How Do You Design the Obvious?

The answer to this question is pretty simple, actually. We already have a list of what makes designs obvious and effective. To define a plan of action for how to create obvious designs, we simply need to turn that list into a list of goals. It'll take the rest of this book to fully illustrate the following goals and how to accomplish them, but this section should give you a solid glimpse into what needs to be done, along with some details about where in this book we'll discuss each point.

Turn qualities into goals

The key to creating great Web-based software is to turn the list of qualities from the preceding section into a list of goals. In other words, our new mission should be to create software that does the following:

- **Conforms to the way users interact with the Web, but focuses on the activity instead of a specific audience.** Understanding users is key to understanding how to approach application design, but as long as we have this understanding, it's best to ignore the demands of users and focus on the activity itself so we can create a feature set that makes sense for the product. In Chapter 2, we'll talk about how to understand users and why it's necessary to ignore their whims.

- **Has only those features that are absolutely necessary for users to complete the activity the application is meant to support.** Moving the "nice to have" features out of the "things to build right now" column is never easy, but it must be done. In Chapter 3, we'll talk about how to divide up the feature list and when to reevaluate nice-to-haves.

- **Supports the user's mental model of what it does.** Allowing an application interface to reflect the inner workings of the program itself is a classic no-no in application design. We'll talk about the differences between implementation models and mental models in Chapter 4 and discuss ways to twist and contort and mold your application into shape before you ever write a single line of code.

- **Helps users get started quickly so they can become intermediate users as soon as possible.** Once users understand how to work with it, the newbie stuff goes away so they can perform their regular operations with ease. Then it eases them into the advanced features. We'll talk about this in Chapter 5.

- **Makes it easy for users to recover from mistakes and difficult to make them in the first place.** Applications should avoid demeaning or interfering with the work of users in any way, instead offering polite interactions that keep things moving forward. Users have enough software issues to deal with—they don't need our modal dialog boxes interrupting their workflow, or error messages popping up to tell them they've screwed something up or that an application has failed in some way. This kind of negative feedback is just plain rude, and reduces a user's ability to explore an application. Software can become more polite, however, through the creation of **poka-yoke** devices. Poka-yoke is the great idea with the funny name. Roughly translated from its Japanese origins, it means "error-proofing." And you'd be surprised how easy it is to create such devices in Web software. We'll talk about this in Chapter 6.

- **Has uniformly designed interface elements, but leverages irregularity to create meaning and importance.** Uniformity is core to good design, but knowing how to leverage irregularity is a little trickier. We'll explore this in Chapter 7.

- **Reduces clutter to a minimum.** Finally, in Chapter 8, we'll examine the concepts of clarity and simplicity in Web design, look at how to eliminate waste in the design process and in our interfaces, and put Just in Time design to work to iteratively create software that does its job well.

With this list of goals spelled out before you, the task of designing the obvious might seem much simpler than it did before. But, as you'd expect, it's much easier to *believe* you know how to do all these things than it is to actually do them. So the rest of this book is all about the things we need to know and do to make these goals a reality.

To get started, let me introduce you to what I affectionately call "The Framework for Obvious Design."

▶ The Framework for Obvious Design

The Framework for Obvious Design is like a 12-step program for people who produce Web-based software, but there are no steps and the number of things to remember is much lower. In fact, there are only three parts.

OK, so it's really more like a three-layer cake.

Each part of the framework is discussed in different contexts throughout this book. The framework isn't broken up into three major sections, each focusing on an individual piece, because it isn't that clear-cut. Each part ties itself up into every aspect of application design, so don't expect to read this section of the book while standing in the bookstore and walk out a genius. You really need to take the book home and read it all the way through.

That said, you may notice the three elements that make up the framework are, in fact, *pretty darn obvious.*

The three parts are as follows:

- Know What to Build

- Know What Makes It Great

- Know the Best Ways to Implement It

It doesn't take a rocket surgeon to realize that knowing these things will result in better products, but for some reason, it can take a long time to see the obvious. It took me about six years.

A key point about this framework is that it will still apply in the future. Not an Ajax guru? Doesn't matter. Don't know the difference between DHTML and XHTML? No biggie. Don't know your JSON from your XML? Fret not. The framework will carry you through. When all these things have come and gone, replaced by bigger and better flavor-of-the-week technologies, the framework will live on, guiding you down the path of Web righteousness.

Also, it's important to understand that nothing in this book related to the *process* of application design is mandated in any way. You can use whatever methods are most effective for you. This book is about the qualities of good Web applications and how to create them. In support of achieving these qualities, I'll tell you about several process-related solutions that work for different people, but you shouldn't feel obligated to adhere to them, nor should you expect to learn about a specific development process in this book that outlines exactly how to create great Web applications any time, any place. Nothing works for everyone, no process works for every application, and no process in the world will tell you what makes applications great. Even the best development processes do not guarantee an application will be good. It's up to you to come up with the million-dollar ideas. I'm just here to tell you how to make them *work*.

To get things started, let's take a quick look at the three major elements of the Framework for Obvious Design.

Know what to build

Knowing what to build requires understanding the purpose of the application and its scope.

With this knowledge, you can build the right tool for the job, whatever that job might be. An application that does a good job of filling a need will be desirable by potential users. Heck, it doesn't even have to fill a need. It could be aimed strictly at having some fun or providing a new approach to an old problem. Whatever the case, knowing the essential ingredients that will allow the application to do its job well will result in a design that is more obvious to users.

To start, the aim is to create an "elevator pitch." When you have 30 seconds to get the attention of your boss or a new client and present a new idea, you have to communicate the idea in a meaningful and attention-getting fashion, with very few words. From there, as long as the initial idea is clear and worth some extra attention, you can elaborate and talk about the target audience and feature set, and try to nail down the essence of the application and how it will work.

The knowledge of what to build, what not to build, and the underlying rationale for the application make up the **conceptual element** of the framework. The conceptual element creates desirability, because applications with a clear purpose that fill a void in an effective manner are always welcome.

Know what makes it great

You already know what makes Web-based software great because you read the list earlier in this chapter.

The list is by no means limited, however. If you discover something else that makes software really good, add it to your list. Just make sure it's a *quality* of the software and not a detail.

For example, drag-and-drop interactions cannot make a Web application great. What makes it great is that the application offers real-time feedback based on user input. (In fact, maybe we should add that to the list now.)

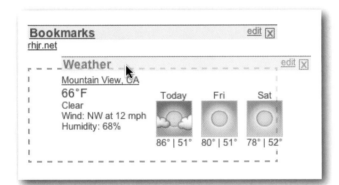

Google Personalized features drag-and-drop content pods that provide a real-time preview so you always know where the pod will land when you let go of it.

These qualities may be hard to spot, so you have to look closely for them. When an application is designed badly, it tells you at every opportunity just how bad it is. But when it's good, you usually can't explain why it's good. You can't put your finger on it, but you know it when you see it.

All these qualities make up the **application element**. They help create a sustainable and positive user experience.

Know the best ways to implement it

This part of the framework is the biggest variable. As we've all seen, the best way to do something usually changes over time.

At one point in history, for example, the best way to have a conversation with someone 100 miles away was to, well, walk there. Later, phones came into play (OK, *much* later). Now, it's as simple as typing a message into an instant messaging program and waiting a moment for the recipient to reply.

Right now, Ajax (Asynchronous Javascript and XML) is all the rage, and coupling it with DHTML has enabled some clever teams to create Web-based applications that do a decent job of emulating desktop applications. Five years ago, this wasn't possible because no one could reliably build a desktop-style interaction for the Web and expect it to work well in all the major browsers. Ten years from now, it will be a whole different story.

Regardless of the best way to implement a particular feature, these tools make up the **interaction element**, which enables the usability of an application and creates what many people call the "X factor." This is the part of the application with which people actually interact.

Throughout this book, I'll discuss ways to implement application elements in such a way that they make operations obvious and effective. I'll also provide some practical examples by showing you how to redesign several typical implementations of Web interface elements so they are more meaningful, more helpful, and more effective.

2

Understand Users, Then Ignore Them

▶ Understand How Users Think They Do Things

▶ Understand How Users Actually Do Things

▶ Know How to Uncover Reality

▶ Design for the Activity

▶ Write Use Cases

Whether or not you want to believe it, the vast majority of software projects fail. They fail to live up to customers' expectations, fail to sufficiently support the activities they were conceived to make easier, and fail to gain the ever-elusive customer loyalty earned by companies like Apple, Google, and Amazon.

Many factors can be blamed for the ultimate failure of a product, but they tend to fall into the same few camps of thought. Sometimes a product fails because it doesn't stand up against the competition. Sometimes it's because the market isn't ready for your product. And sometimes it's because users just don't get what you were trying to do.

Of course, none of these complaints are the *real* reason. Sometimes the failure of a product doesn't seem to make any sense at all. Sometimes your product has all the same features as the other guy's product—and then some—and it still fails to capture the market the way its competitors have. Sometimes users understand completely what the tool is supposed to do but choose another one anyway. You ask yourself over and over, Why? Why can't my product do every bit as well as my competitor's?

There is no single answer. But some of them go like this:

- Typically, users latch on to the first Web site or tool they find that they can tolerate, and they stick to it. Most of the time users spend on the Web isn't devoted to visiting new sites and discovering new things. Rather, users go to the same sites over and over. And you haven't given them a good enough reason to switch.

- Your product isn't better than the competition's just because you crammed more features into it (more about this in Chapter 3). Your long list of features may make for good marketing material, but it also adds up to complicated software that confuses and frustrates users. Most users never become experts who benefit from the more advanced features. The majority of users, in fact, become interme-diate-level users quickly, and stay at that level as long as they use the product. I'll discuss this point further in Chapter 5.

- The difficulty of accomplishing tasks in your application means that users don't stick around to fight their way through it, and they don't bother coming back.

Whatever the reason (and there are plenty more to go around), the most important point is that you need to know—at the very beginning of your project—*what to build*, and why. With that knowledge, you can overcome potential causes for failure and build an application that serves its users effectively. To start, you need to know a few things about how people really work with the Web. Much of this chapter is about how to find out how people really work so you can design things that work for them. Later, however, we'll talk about the benefits of largely *ignoring* users and focusing your design efforts on supporting a specific activity.

▶ Understand How Users Think They Do Things

A few weeks ago, I heard an interesting story that did a nice job of revealing the differences between how people think they act and how they actually act. The story was about a new sandwich from a fast-food restaurant.

See, the marketers did lots of research before releasing the idea upon the public. They asked a bunch of people if they would find appealing the idea of ordering a low-carb version of their hottest-selling cheeseburger. Resoundingly, people said they would, indeed, love to take their usual trip to the establishment and order something they know is good for them and their families. The marketers knew they were on to something. So they whipped up a plan, sent the recipe-makers into action, and released the sandwich, sure that their hours of hard work would pay off and earn the company big dividends.

Reality kicked in a short while later. The sandwich failed miserably and quickly disappeared from the menu.

Why, you ask?

People often don't do what they think they would do. They don't act the way they think they would act. We can talk for hours about how we would respond in any given situation, but we don't really know what will happen when the hypothetical becomes real. The sandwich failed to live up to its promise because the promise was based on meaningless conversations with people who thought they would do the smart, responsible thing and make the healthy choice.

The marketers, I'm sure, didn't mean to have meaningless conversations. It's more likely that they asked leading questions, such as "Would you choose to eat the healthier version when given the choice?" It's a question designed to make the person who says, "No, I wouldn't" feel like an idiot for doing so. It's a question designed to get a "Yes, I would."

And even if the questions were presented in an unbiased way, you can't just walk up to people on the street and ask them what they would do. No one really knows what he or she would do. History shows us that people don't always make the right choices. They make comfortable choices. They make safe choices. More to the point, they make the choices they *know how to make*.

It's difficult to predict how we'd make decisions in hypothetical situations. Hardly anyone can do this well. When we intentionally begin making better choices, we usually do so in increments, making small improvements for a short time. At some point we find ourselves in a stressful situation and immediately revert. We fall back on the types of choices we've been making our whole lives. The ones we know how to make.

One kid starts screaming or crying, another starts begging ruthlessly for a kid's meal with the shiny new toy from his new favorite cartoon movie, and the money in hand goes toward whatever will get them to settle down. Forget the healthy sandwich, just give me one kid's meal, please.

When people use computers, it's usually because they need to accomplish something. Your application stands between them and their mission. And while many people who use the Web regularly feel pretty confident with it, we all know someone—someone close—who can never quite figure out whether or not the one-click purchase they just made on Amazon.com is going to ship to the new house or the old one.

Every time I'm about to make a one-click purchase on Amazon, I make about 20 other superfluous clicks first so I can double-check the address and credit card information Amazon has on file. Of course, if someone from Amazon asked me if I would use the one-click checkout, I'd say yes. I wouldn't admit to the 20 other clicks, because I prefer to believe I can trust the one-click check-out process enough to be sure my order will be shipped to me correctly.

I don't feel comfortable making a one-click purchase on Amazon.com, because I don't trust the one-click settings (which means the design is a little *too* obvious). But I'd never admit that to an Amazon usability specialist if he asked me outright.

People prefer to think they know how they would act in any given situation. But very few of them chose the low-carb cheeseburger.

You can't ask users outright what they want. You get theoretical answers. You don't get the answers that result from real choices in real situations. You don't get the truth about how people think and work.

Now you know.

▶ Understand How Users Actually Do Things

People are funny. Especially when it comes to using computers.

Instead of becoming gurus of the applications we use every day, we tend to learn about 20 percent or so of what the application is capable of doing.

Sometimes we even intentionally hide some or all of the other 80 percent of features (if we can figure out how to hide them), or at least ignore them, because they get in the way.

When I started writing this book, for example, I hid every last tool Microsoft Word has to offer except for the Zoom tool. I also kept the custom Styles toolbar, which New Riders authors need to format books in a consistent fashion. But I don't need all the other tools Word offers because I know the keyboard shortcuts for the things I do regularly, like make text **bold**, *italicize* it, or <u>underline</u> it. I also know how to create new documents and save the ones I'm working on. There are keyboard shortcuts for all these things; the toolbar that offers these commands, via some cute little icons, just takes up space. As a result, I have nothing on my screen but this document, the Styles toolbar, which takes up very little room over on the right, and the Zoom tool, which shows only the percentage at which I am currently zoomed, and is displayed nicely in a drop-down menu that enables me to change the zoom level at any time.

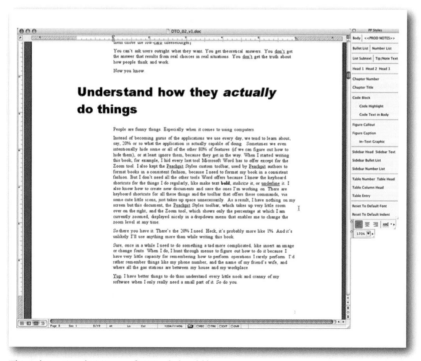

This is how simple Microsoft Word *should* be.

So there you have it. There's the 20 percent I need. Heck, it's probably more like 1 percent. And it's unlikely I'll use anything more while writing this book.

Sure, once in a while I'll need to do something a tad more complicated, like insert an image or change fonts. When I do, I'll hunt through menus to figure out how, because I have very little capacity for remembering how to perform operations I rarely perform. I'd rather remember things like my phone number, and the name of my friend's wife, and where all the gas stations are between my house and my workplace.

Yup. I have better things to do than understand every little nook and cranny of my software when I only really need a small part of it. So do you.

Want to know a secret? Our users are just like us. They have things to do as well. Loads of things. They don't have time to comprehend every nook and cranny either.

Humbling, isn't it? For all the time and energy we put into creating robust applications that do everything but wash the dishes, only a very small percentage of people ever even venture into the nooks and crannies. They stick to the 20 percent (or less) that they need, and they rarely advance their skills. (There are exceptions to this, of course, but I'll talk about that later on.)

People also tend to learn one way to use their application and stick to it. Some prefer menus, some prefer icons, and of course, some prefer keyboard shortcuts. Very few of these people bother remembering more than one way to complete a task beyond those basic operations (in which case, they might know two or three methods). And why should they? Is there any benefit to knowing more than one way to change a tire? No, not really.

Mental models

Another noticeable behavioral tendency is that people form an opinion about how something works and latch onto it. For example, my wife recently divulged to me that Word is much better for creating tables for printed documents than Microsoft Excel. This surprised me. My wife is a smart, computer-savvy woman who teaches computer classes twice a week as part of her job as head librarian for a local library, so I didn't doubt that what she was telling me was accurate, but it surprised me nonetheless.

Excel is a spreadsheet program. Word is a word processor. When I think of creating a table, to present tabular data, for printing or otherwise, I think of Excel. But my wife thinks of Excel as a giant calculator, and Word as a word processor with a cunning ability to create tables that print the way she needs them to print.

Huh.

My wife is what she and I would both call an "expert user." I am not. I don't spend a lot of time using Word, and when I do, I use it for basic tasks (you know, like writing a book). I don't know my way around it nearly as well as she does. The same is true for Excel. Equations are not my forte. If the tiny calculator application that comes with my operating system isn't enough to do what I need, then as far as I'm concerned, I'm in over my head.

The point here is that I have an average user's understanding of Word. And in my mental model, it's a word processor. Nothing more, nothing less. When I need to process words, that's where I go. When I need a table, I go to Excel. Like most people, I use these tools for the purposes I think they're best equipped to handle.

I also have my own ideas about how these tools work. When I save a document, I believe Word is taking all the changes I've made since the last time I saved the document and is saving them to that file on my desktop (or wherever the file might live). I also think the document I'm looking at is the same thing as the file on my desktop. Which, I guess, means I'm looking at the document in one place while the changes I make to it are being saved to another place. Thus my "mental model" (what I *believe* to be true) of a document requires that it exist in two places simultaneously. This sounds pretty silly. (I'll talk more about mental models, and how they play into our ability to design the obvious, in Chapter 4.)

I know that what's actually happening is that a bunch of ones and zeros that live on my hard drive are keeping all this data I've entered intact so I can recover it at will, and all I'm seeing on the screen is a graphical rendering of the ones and zeros. Technically, the characters on the screen aren't even characters. But it doesn't matter.

All I care about—all I ever need to know—is that pressing Ctrl/Cmd + S saves the changes I've made to the document. That tiny bit of information is enough to get me through the fog of modern word processing. It's how I think Word works, and it's the only thought that matters to me.

All this applies to users' behavior on the Web, as well. That is, people using Web applications also tend to do the following:

- Learn 20 percent or so of what an application can do

- Learn one way to do something and stick to it

- Form their own understanding about how applications work

Ironically, people tend to wish the applications they use had other features. More features. Features that would, according to the comments that riddle blogs and forums all over the Web, compel some people to do all sorts of crazy things, like "pay twice as much if only the software did *this*," or "get my entire company to switch to this application if only it did *that*."

So how do you find out what users *really* need?

▶ Know How to Uncover Reality

The way to uncover the reality of what users really want and need should seem obvious. After all, if you're like the rest of us, you've had at least one argument in your life about whether you were listening to your spouse, your parents, your best friend, or [*insert person here*].

But it's not obvious at all.

When we communicate with our spouses, we have a history to rely on. We know how to talk to and listen to our spouses. Our users, on the other hand, are alien to us. We have no history with them, we've never hung out with them at a bar on a Friday night, and we don't typically have long conversations over dinner with them. So when we're faced with trying to understand what our users really need, it's very easy to forget everything we know about communicating with other people.

For example, if I were designing and building an application used to track sales trends for the Sales department in my own company, my first instinct, if I decided to research my users, would be to hunt down Molly from Sales and ask her what she would like the application to do. Tell me, Molly, how should the Sales Trends Odometer display the data you need?

I would never ask my father—someone I have history with—the same type of question. My father knows next to nothing about how Web sites are built, what complicated technologies lie lurking beneath the pretty graphics, or the finer points of information architecture. He wouldn't even be able to pick a Web application out of a lineup, because he doesn't understand what I mean by the word *application*. Is Amazon.com an application? He doesn't know. He just knows it's a Web page and he bought a book there once.

What my father does know is that the model rockets he builds for fun on weekends require several parts that he has to hunt down on a regular basis.

He has to make sure he gets to the model rocket store on time every week so he has the parts he needs to complete his rockets, so he can head off to the airstrip and boost a few with his friends. (These are big, professional-level rockets that are often upwards of 8 feet tall and use small explosives as engines. The Federal Aviation Administration regulates the launching of such rockets because they can fly high enough to actually hit planes that have recently taken off; hence the need to use an actual airstrip.)

If I told my dad he could buy these parts online, he'd be interested. If I asked him how the application should filter the online catalog and allow him to make purchases, he'd look at me like I was nuts.

Molly from Sales would likely do the same thing.

Molly has no idea what your software might be able to do, and she almost certainly doesn't have the technical chops to explain it. She likely doesn't realize that your product could make the task of creating a client birthday list (for mailing out discount coupons) a matter of two clicks, and therefore, she would never mention that this task is particularly gruesome and ask if your software could do it for her. Thus, you need to look a little deeper to find out what Molly needs.

If you want to know what Molly wants the software to do, don't ask her directly. Instead, find out what she does, how she does it, and *what she will want to do later*. Eventually, you'll figure out how all that translates into a Web application. For now, don't think about Web applications. Think about users.

Assume nothing

There are several ways to uncover what's most important to the people who use (or will use) your applications. The first way is simply to assume you know what your users want, how they work with computers, and how your application will fare under their nimble, Web-savvy fingertips. I don't recommend this approach.

If you want to know how users work, don't assume anything. Almost on a daily basis, my wife encounters a customer in her library who has entered his email address into the Address bar in Internet Explorer and is wondering why he can't check his email. A few days ago, she told me about someone who added *.com* to the end of his username for his Web-mail program and wanted to know why he couldn't access his home computer. If only it were so simple!

These people are not dumb, by any means. Some of these people are business owners, managers, organizers, and stellar employees. They're experts at something. But they are new to using computers and don't yet understand how to interact with them.

You probably don't know these people. You are surrounded by people who know the Web extremely well because they spend most of their time building it. And you are probably surprised to hear that the less computer-savvy among us can have such a difficult time performing basic operations. But these people are real, and they might one day use *your* application. Don't assume you know anything about them without finding out firsthand. The second you do, someone will come along and ask why he can't scan his printed document by holding it up to the monitor. (Yes, this has happened.)

Use surveys

An effective way to find people who fall into your target user category is to survey people doing the job your application is meant to support. If you're developing a sales support tool, for example, look to your own company's sales department. Put together a quick screening survey and send it out to the whole department to determine who might have the most useful information. If your product is aimed more at senior salespeople, the survey should weed out the trainees and leave you with a shortlist of qualified sales veterans.

SurveyMonkey.com makes quick work of creating nice, easy-to-use survey forms, and it offers a set of tools to analyze the results. I highly recommend it, but you can use whatever survey tool makes you happy and gives you the information you need.

Surveys are effective for acquiring high-level information; for example, they can help you determine satisfaction levels in regard to an existing application, or poll people about how they do their jobs. It's difficult to pinpoint what

Question Type
Select the **type of question** from the list below.

Choice - One Answer (Vertical)

Question
Enter the text for your question below.

What type of information do you collect most often using SurveyMonkey?

☐ **Answer Required Customize...**
☐ **Randomize Choices**

Answer Choices
Enter each choice on separate lines below.

Customer satisfaction levels
Task difficulty ratings
I don't own a monkey

Check the box below to add an "other" field. The respondent will be allowed to enter a different answer than the choices you've provided.

☐ Other (please specify)   Single Line

Rely on SurveyMonkey.com as a tool to more fully understand your target user.

areas cause the most trouble for users or which ones take the most time, but surveys can help you gather information about how people rate the overall usability of an application, what they like best about it, what they like least, what part of their job takes the most time, and so on. You shouldn't expect to learn the subtle details of how a person interacts with the shopping cart on a site, but you can gather focus-group–style information pretty easily.

Contextual inquiry

Contextual inquiry is an abbreviated version of ethnographic research, in which the researcher lives and works with people in a particular culture with the intent of learning about them from an inside perspective.

Most of us don't have the time, will power, or energy to go live and work with a bunch of accountants so we can better understand how to build an effective Web-based invoicing system. But we can perform ethnographic research on a smaller scale, in the form of short, "shadow"-style interview sessions known as contextual inquiry. The idea behind contextual inquiry is to observe target users on their own turf so you can see how they *really* do things. I find this method especially useful when the people I'm observing are already using an existing version of the application I'm working to improve.

For example, I once worked on an application that was meant to support the development of nonlinear e-learning courseware. The application was supposed to show learners a version of a course that was customized according to their input during different sections of the course. (That is, if a user answered a question about a particular topic incorrectly, the next set of screens might focus more heavily on that topic, whereas users who chose the correct answer would not see this set of screens, instead moving directly to the next section.)

The initial users for this application were internal employees, as the company had a group of instructional designers on hand to create audio scripts and guidelines for the company's courseware. Thus there were daily opportunities for contextual inquiry, and endless amounts of quality information could be extracted from simple conversations with those users. This application had no road map at all—no design work had been done to plot it out—so contextual inquiry became a primary method for determining how to evolve the tool. Most of us working on the application had no experience as instructional designers, and the best way to understand how to create the application was to get to know the people who did instructional design for a living.

To find out how well people handled the simple task of accessing a course that had already been created with the tool so it could be edited, I could simply walk over to an instructor's desk and ask a question about how she had set up a particular course. She would open up the application, navigate to the course I was asking about, and give me a guided tour. From watching the user perform that sequence of operations, I could clearly see where the tool was giving her trouble and make mental notes about what was difficult about it.

There's nothing complicated about contextual inquiry. It's just a matter of hanging out with a few users for a while to see how they work, how they think, what issues arise while they're working, how they make decisions, and, ultimately, how they interact with your application so you can see how effective or ineffective it really is.

At the interaction level, if a user is interrupted by a phone call in the middle of a complicated task, is it easy for him to jump right back into the task when the call has ended? Can he move quickly to another part of the tool (perhaps to check a setting) and come back without missing a beat? If this happens, why does it happen? How can the application address this need?

At the application level, is the tool meeting the user's expectations? Does it behave the way she thinks it will, or does she often end up muttering at her screen while trying to understand what just happened? Is the tool well organized, making things easy for her to find? What types of things is she doing repeatedly, and are those things easy to get to on a frequent basis?

Contextual inquiry can actually be very similar to usability testing. The key difference is that the users being observed are working in their own environments, at their own desks, dealing with all the things they deal with during a normal workday, including manipulating several applications at once.

If a version of your application is not in use yet, contextual inquiry can be effective for determining what things a tool still in the conceptual phase needs to do so, you can *Know What To Build.*

Shadowing

If you're a programmer, the last thing you want to do is talk to those peppy salespeople down the hall who ring a big gong every time they make a sale. But if your product is aimed at salespeople, try to find a few who don't completely clash with you and latch onto them. These folks are your users, and they have the most information about how their jobs are done and what they need to know to do it well. If you're building a product for a client company and can't simply wander down the hall to perform such inquiries, make arrangements to spend a few days at the company so you can talk to users there and learn what you can on-site.

Set up a time to **shadow** several users individually, and go have some fun bonding with your new best friends. Shadowing is the act of quietly hovering over the shoulder of someone who knows what they're doing, with the goal of learning to do that person's job so that you may one day also become a Jedi Master. Contextual inquiry is really just a fancy name for shadowing.

Shadowing doesn't have to be overly formal. In fact, the more rapport you have with the users you observe, the more likely they are to open up and tell you about the things they struggle with all the time—things your application can help resolve.

Naturally, there are a few tricks to shadowing. You can't just waltz in and expect someone to tell you exactly what the application needs to do.

- First, make it abundantly clear that you are not trying to build a tool that replaces them; you're trying to build a tool that makes their jobs easier. You certainly don't want your users thinking you're stealthily finding ways to make them homeless for the holidays.

- Next, follow them around and see what it is they do and how they do it. Take notes using a notepad and a pen. Although it's ridiculously low tech, it's still the best way to write quick notes when you're running around.

- Ask questions, but not so many that you become a major distraction. Just ask simple questions to clarify anything that isn't perfectly clear.

- As you're doing all this, quietly think of all the ways a good application could eliminate Redundant Task A, Annoying Task B, and I Hate This Part of My Job Task C.

- Keep things casual and light. Spend a day with one or two people, or half a day with each of several people. If time is tight, spend two hours with five or six people over a two-day period and stop there.

- Try doing the job your application is supposed to support. This is a fantastic way to uncover reality. No one can explain the finer points better than you can after actually dealing with them directly for a while. Putting yourself on the firing line gives you incredible insights in a very short time. This idea can also be applied later by "eating your own dog food" (that is, using your own products), which I'll discuss in Chapter 4.

Remote-user research

If you don't have direct access to your users—perhaps because you are building commercial software meant to be used by millions of people, none of whom work within 100 yards of your desk, and you can't visit your client's site—you can perform remote research and gain some of the same insights using Web-based tools like WebEx and GoToMeeting, or by making a few simple phone calls to some of your customers.

You won't get the same in-depth knowledge you would from contextual inquiry, and the environment will be less natural than if you were stalking a coworker in person for a day. But you can still get information that helps you build an organizational structure and feature set that make sense for your application by interviewing people over the phone about what they do, or by having them perform tasks in the current version of your application or a related product and taking notes about how they work, what trips them up, and what you can do to help them. (But don't make any promises. Promises backfire big-time when whatever it is you promised doesn't make it into the next release.)

To persona or not to persona?

Alan Cooper, author of *The Inmates Are Running the Asylum*, posits that a great way to keep the goals of your users in mind is by creating a **persona** for each one. A persona, at its core, is a user profile focused on goals and activities rather than demographics, where each fictitious user has a name, photo, and some personal details that bring him or her to life. The basic idea is that attaching a name and face to the very flexible notion of a user helps lock down who the user really is, making him less open to interpretation when it comes time to decide whether or not the real users out there will be able to decipher how the Data-Juicer application works.

Personas are also meant to help programmers realize that the person on the other side of the screen is not made of rubber, and cannot be bent at random to fit arbitrary ideas of what a user can handle and will find useful. Programmers and managers alike are forced to acknowledge that Molly from Sales may not really understand how the word *publish* translates to pushing her unfinished content to the intranet where the whole company can see it.

A persona doesn't have to be anything complicated. The description can be as short as a single paragraph or as long as, um, two or three paragraphs. The important part is that it describes a fictitious user who represents the real people who will be using your product, how savvy they are, how and why they'll be using the product, and so on, topped off with a couple of fictitious personal details, a name, and a photo. (The photos don't need to be high quality. The inexpensive, low-resolution versions from any stock photography site will do just fine. You can get them for just a couple of bucks on sites like **iStockphoto.com**, or Getty Images, at **www.getty-images.com**.)

Even if your product will be used by a wide range of people, it's not necessary to create a persona for every single user type. When it comes to the particular activity your product is meant to support, the problems of one group will often be extremely similar to the problems of the others. In fact, using too many personas is counterproductive because you end up trying to please everyone, which is not usually possible.

The goal is to narrow your list of user types down to three or four—preferably fewer—and create a persona for each of them. One in particular should serve as your primary persona—the one that absolutely must be satisfied for your product to be a success.

Throughout the rest of your design and development process, Cooper recommends keeping the personas in front of everyone involved, all the time. Everyone on the development team should know the users—let's call them Greg, Anna, and Mary—well enough to know exactly how they're likely to respond when faced with a complicated interaction.

For example, if you're designing a stock photography Web site, one of your personas might be described like this:

Greg is a 26-year-old print designer from San Jose, California. He has extensive experience with tools like Adobe Photoshop and Illustrator. He has very little experience designing for the Web, but has been picking up more and more Web projects in recent weeks and would like to expand his skills. His design work, which often includes ads for trade magazines and brochures, has won several awards, and he is comfortable using stock photography sites, particularly Getty Images, where he frequently purchases high-resolution photographs. His No. 1 pet peeve with such stock photography sites is the time it takes to wade through thousands of images to find exactly what he needs.

This persona is Greg the Print Designer.

This simple description of the fictitious user Greg reveals several key points. First, Greg is comfortable with computers and the Internet and wants to focus more on Web design. Second, as a contractor, his time is probably limited, making it even more frustrating to wade through thousands of images to find what he needs. Third, he needs high-quality images so he can continue winning awards.

Pleasing Greg is critical to the success of your stock photography site. Despite being relatively new to Web design, he will be taking on Web projects more and more, and he would love to have a one-stop shop online for all the images he needs. Greg could be a loyal, frequent customer if you design something that works well for him.

To address Greg's time constrains, you can do several things in the interface. First, you can point out which images, or which versions of an image are suitable for the Web by including the file size within the image information and perhaps a small icon that makes Web-ready images easy to spot. You could also provide links to relevant supporting material on the site to educate Greg—for example, articles about the differences between images on the Web and those intended for print work.

Next, you can create a way for Greg to save the searches he performs, and a way to store groups of images in a personal library so he can quickly access personalized categories of images and find the ones he likes more easily. This will save Greg huge amounts of time in the long run. When he first begins to use the site, he'll have to wade through images as he does on other stock sites, but each time he does so, he can add the images he likes to his library, even if he doesn't use them right away. The more he uses the site, the larger his library will grow, and the more he'll be able to find images he likes quickly.

These few features will help Greg a lot, and the simple act of writing out a description of who he is has helped you take a big leap toward designing an effective application.

But one part of the feature set is still a concern: the first several times Greg uses the site, he still has to wade through tons of images, just as he would on any other site, and it may be difficult for him to see the benefit of having a personal library during the first three or four visits. We know Greg is already using other stock photography sites, and he may be hesitant to start digging through a new one, so you need to give him a good reason to switch—and make the shift immediately beneficial. This issue might have never surfaced if you hadn't gotten to know Greg.

Now that you know him, you can address this issue by offering him ten free images in the first month, and guide him toward adding images to his library during each of his first few visits. (I'll talk about how to get people up to speed with an application in Chapter 5.) While browsing for his ten free images, he'll start adding images to his library, and by the time he's used all his free photos, he'll have built up a small arsenal that he can use in the future. Now you've given Greg a reason to visit, a way to personalize what he sees on repeat visits, and a reason to keep him coming back.

Greg's happy. You're happy.

As you can see, having a persona like Greg by your side during the design process can be really helpful when you're starting to narrow down the feature list for an application. You know Greg, you know what his goals are as a designer, and as a result, you Know What To Build. You can refer back to the persona again and again to keep yourself in check when considering new features.

Greg is not real, of course, but you can leverage what you now know about your users as a result of personifying them through Greg, so you have a better idea of what to leave in, what to leave out, when to walk away, and when to run.

The theoretical benefits

Personas are a vital part of what is known as **Goal-Directed Design**, a process developed by Alan Cooper to help designers better understand the goals of users so interactive systems can be designed to help them meet those goals.

The essence of Goal-Directed Design is to try to break down the wall that exists between our users and us. As a metaphor, consider a conversation between a developer and a user. The developer explains how and why something happens, and the user nods his head and says, "I don't care how it happened, or why—I just want to know it's fixed so I can move on with my life."

Developers tend to want to put up dialog boxes and error messages and all sorts of intrusive widgets that explain what's going on behind the scenes, but users don't care. They only want to know the thing is working so they can accomplish their goals.

A user's goals live outside the application. The goals are personal. Very few users have a goal of understanding how PeopleSoft works. That goal is usually encapsulated by a larger goal. Perhaps Molly wants to earn a promotion at work and thinks that understanding PeopleSoft better will enable her to be more productive. The application itself is not a goal at all—it's an obstacle between Molly and her goal.

Acknowledging that the user's goals have nothing to do with your Web application allows you to design something that pays more attention to the user's real goals. Thus, Goal-Directed Design involves performing thorough user research, creating personas through which to gauge how well a design holds up, and designing something that works for the target users, in the context in which they use the application. Goal-Directed Design means listening to users, getting to the truth of what they want, and creating applications from a more informed perspective.

The reality

Goal-Directed Design can be very effective, and it's a process used by many successful designers. That said, it seems to work best when the application being designed is intended for a niche audience: It's much easier to establish a core set of users when the user base is fairly narrow at the start. Trying to execute Goal-Directed Design when your application is to be used by millions of people across a wide array of user types may not produce the results you need.

Furthermore, personas are meant to be used in conjunction with *scenarios*, which are essentially short stories about how a persona might interact with the system designed for her. And it's at this point that the practicality of using personas starts to become a little . . . fuzzy.

I, for one, am no character actor. I can't easily pretend to be someone else— not in any realistic way. And I can't safely predict how I, as this other person, would handle the interactions laid out before me as a shiny, new Web application, or whether or not the application would even be interesting to me.

When you start imagining how a fictitious character would respond to a hypothetical situation using an imaginary interface, it's probably time to put down your little plastic army men and crack open the sketchbook.

We can do the research, get to know our users on a personal level, and dream up something we think will work very well for our intended users, but time spent on fiction will eventually begin to interfere with reality. When the fuzzy starts to get too fuzzy, it's time to start moving toward something tangible.

▶ Design for the Activity

There's one last thing you should understand about people before you run off to create surveys and plan contextual inquiries. And it's the fact that really changes things. It's the fact that makes it possible to design the obvious.

You ready?

People adapt to technology.

I know—it's surprising. But think about your average day. You wake up to a digital alarm clock, use the remote control to turn on the television, hit the start button on the coffeemaker, push another little button to open the garage door, get in your car and fidget with the stereo while hooking your Apple iPod up to it, and drive to work glancing at the speedometer, gas gauge, and iPod controls the whole time. Then you get to work and log in to your computer, where you crank out email, code, Web pages, whatever, until it's time to go home. Once there, you set the DVR to record your favorite show while you make dinner on a stove full of timers and heat settings, simultaneously answering your cell phone so your spouse can tell you he or she is running late.

You've adapted nicely to all these things. You may have had to read a manual or two along the way, but you figured them out at some point, got them up and running, and now you don't even have to think about how these things work. What this tells us is that it's possible to design things that support the needs of your users without knowing anything about their goals and dreams and ambitions and other things movies are made of.

Cars, alarm clocks, stereos, stove-tops, and millions of other devices have been developed almost entirely without the aid of Goal-Directed Design. This is because there are plenty of designers in the world who believe it's possible to design great products without researching users. For this, I commend them. Goal-Directed Design isn't for everyone.

Sure, personas have their upsides, like the fact that having a strong understanding of your target users can help you see more easily what features and functionality might really help them. But thorough user research is time-consuming; I've personally never worked on a project with a long enough time line that user research could be done *at all*. Most projects are quick, dirty, and painful. Entire Web-based email applications are often designed and built in six weeks instead of six months, and believe me, six weeks is not enough time to learn anything about your users. You're usually far too busy cranking out wireframes.

It's nice when you have the option of getting up close and personal with users, but usually you don't. Time constraints, budgets, lack of interest, and many other factors get in the way almost every single time. And even if it is an option, listening to your loudest users too much often results, ironically, in products that are more difficult for everyone else to use.

To remedy this, we need to trust ourselves to design good Web applications without listening too closely to our users. And renowned user-experience master Donald Norman has just the solution. It's called **Activity-Centered Design**.

Norman's article "Human-Centered Design Considered Harmful" (http://www.jnd.org/dn.mss/human-centered.html) points out that many technologies and products have become great not as a result of a deep understanding of users, but rather because of a "deep understanding of the activities that were to be performed." He cites everything from clocks to musical instruments as examples of products designed only through an understanding of the activities they were meant to support. He states the following:

> One concern is that the focus upon individual people
> (or groups) might improve things for them at the cost
> of making it worse for others. The more something is
> tailored for the particular likes, dislikes, skills, and needs
> of a particular target population, the less likely it will be
> appropriate for others.

His insight is both fascinating and true. Many Web applications have been designed to accommodate niche markets with specific needs, and while many of them are quite successful in their respective markets, Web applications are often, in fact, more successful when they are driven by an authoritative, take-charge designer who almost completely ignores users. And this phenomenon extends well beyond the Web world. Apple's iPod, the most widely adopted portable music player in the world, was designed without a thorough understanding of its users. It was designed to support the activity of listening to music on the go. In the same article Norman states the following:

> *Sometimes what is needed is a design dictator who says, "Ignore what users say: I know what's best for them."*
>
> *The case of Apple Computer is illustrative. Apple's products have long been admired for ease of use. Nonetheless, Apple replaced its well-known, well-respected human interface design team with a single, authoritative (dictatorial) leader. Did usability suffer? On the contrary: its new products are considered prototypes of great design.*

Granted, not everyone has the vision and design chops of Apple's fearless leader, Steve Jobs, but regardless, understanding the activity itself can lead to creating products that support not only a niche audience, but also the public at large.

37signals, the small company with the giant buzz responsible for products like Basecamp and Backpack, is another great example of this. In the case of Basecamp, they saw that project management software was largely about organization and structure and planning, and decided instead to build a project management system that focuses on *communication* through the use of collaborative tools like a message board, file manager, to-do-list, and a dashboard view of recent activity. They felt that charts and graphs didn't really speak to those involved in a project, and users might be better empowered by being allowed to communicate their actual thoughts with other team members via the Web.

If you're familiar with Basecamp, you probably know they were right. Even if you don't like it or use it, many thousands of people are using Basecamp because it supports the activity of management, not the concept of management. The boys at 37signals didn't have the time to research users at great lengths (they actually didn't need to, because they originally built Basecamp for themselves)—they had projects to manage and built something that effectively supported that activity. By doing so, they satisfied their own needs as a business and have made countless others more productive as a result. They designed around an activity and enabled thousands of potentially very different user types to work within the parameters of the activity.

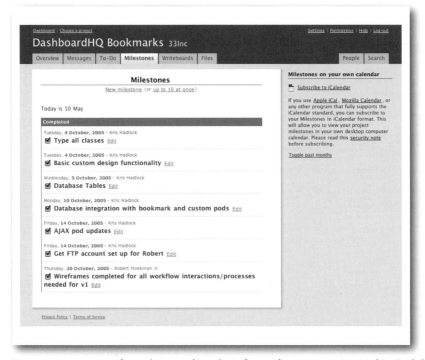

Basecamp steers away from charts and graphs in favor of communication in plain English.

Norman's article doesn't offer much insight about how to gain such a rich understanding of an individual activity, but it does illustrate very well that one does not need a thorough knowledge of users to design products that work for them.

It's easy to see how the same conclusion can be drawn from understanding the activity of searching for and purchasing stock photography online, the example in my discussion of Goal-Directed Design. Anyone who has used online stock images knows it's cumbersome at best to troll through the millions of images on any one site, and some creative thinking could very easily have produced the same feature list as that abstracted from the persona about Greg, the print designer with an increasing number of Web projects.

Activity-Centered Design is effective from the beginning, as the team starts with a construct—an activity—that the application must support. The team then focuses its efforts on the more practical aspects of design by breaking down the activity into a collection of tasks. Tasks are tangible. You can design ways to complete them without knowing anything about your users. Norman continues (in his second article on Activity-Centered Design, located at http://www.jnd.org/dn.mss/hcd_harmful_a_clari.html):

> *Tasks are situations with a single, well-specified goal, such as 'respond to this email.' Activities are larger groupings, comprised of multiple tasks that fit together, such as 'get caught up on the day's correspondence' which means reading email, responding, looking up information, sometimes to copy and paste into emails, checking calendars, and other associated, related tasks.*

Task-flow diagrams

Norman advocates the use of task-flow diagrams. So do I.

A **task-flow diagram** is a flowchart that details how a user will complete all the tasks in an application from beginning to end. Drawing up such a diagram can put you on the path toward an obvious design, because an effective task design is one that makes it obvious how to get from one step to the next in a process, and that process follows an obvious logic.

The diagram below is an example of how a typical shopping experience might go on an e-commerce site. In the diagram, the user wants to buy a desk lamp. To complete the task, the user needs to go to the Products section, drill down into the Desk Lamps category within the Products section, locate a particular desk lamp, add it to the shopping cart, and check out.

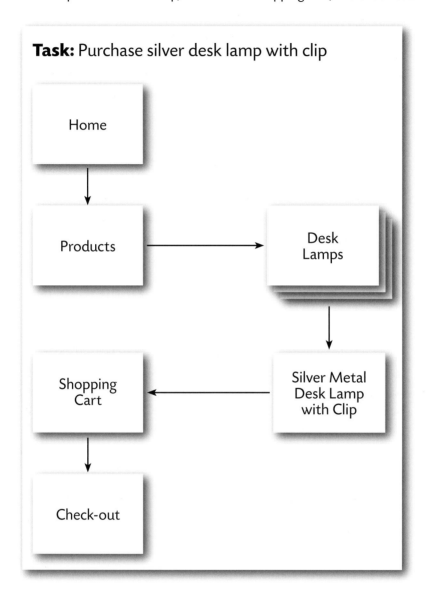

The task-flow diagram not only details how the task will be completed in the application, it also can be used as the basis for a prototype later on. And prototypes can be helpful in usability tests to determine how well the design guides users through the process. (I'll talk about prototypes and usability tests in Chapter 4.)

▶ Write Use Cases

When you're ready to start creating something tangible, a **use case** is an excellent way to capture the workflow that you will eventually build into an application. A use case is a set of step-by-step instructions for how an interaction or a task might be accomplished. You may have heard the term use-case thrown around in your office a few times, and may even understand what it means. If you're a programmer, you probably know better than most, as use cases are often written to explain a procedure before writing the code, to bring it to life.

A use case can be kept at a high-level, describing general situations in which the application will be used (for example, Mary goes to Target.com to create a list of furniture items needed for her new home office), or it can include more detailed descriptions of what actually happens on the screen when each operation is performed and how the user interacts with the user-interface controls along the way.

Faster than code and capable of producing real results

Writing use cases is, perhaps strangely, one of my favorite things to do. In five to 30 minutes, typically, I can list out the exact process for how an interaction will work once it is built. This exercise invariably exposes potential problems and brings to light any assumptions I was making about a task prior to writing it. It also provides a common ground for the developers and myself. When we communicate through use cases, we're speaking the same language, and that's a good thing.

Just yesterday, in fact, I wrote a use case for a task that enables users to submit personal recommendations for products. To do this, I wrote out several steps that looked like this:

Write a Recommendation

Step 1.   User clicks the Write a Recommendation text link, and a short form is displayed immediately beneath the button. Tech note: This form resides in a hidden DIV and loads with the rest of the page.

Step 2. User completes the form.

Step 3. User clicks **OK** to submit the recommendation, and the form disappears.

Then I thought to myself, that doesn't sound right. If the form just disappears as soon as you click **OK**, the user would have no idea whether or not the recommendation was successfully submitted. So I revised Step 3, opting to keep the form visible after clicking **OK**, and displaying a message above the form to tell the user the submission was successful. Then I realized that there would have to be a way to close the form once the user was done with it. So I added a fourth step, in which the user clicks a **Close** button. But I had to decide where to put the button. I asked myself, Should I make a new button and display it as part of the form? Nah, I think I'd rather make the **Write a Recommendation** link toggle based on context. This link can't be used once the form is displayed, for obvious reasons, so instead of disabling it and displaying another button for the **Close** action, why not reuse **Write a Recommendation** in a new context? Once you click that button, its label and function could *change* to a **Close** button. If I combine the two buttons, I enable the user to open and close the form without moving the mouse (should the user decide not to complete the form, that is).

So, great, now I have a four-step use case that says the user will click the button, complete the form, click **OK** to submit the form, and click **Close** to make the form go away (optional). I now have a single button that has two purposes, the user has access to the form right in the page instead of being sent to another page in a round-trip process, and the whole interaction is "as simple as possible, but not simpler" (Albert Einstein). Perfect. That's my use case.

Wait. What happens if the user decides not to complete the form?

Writing exceptions

Exceptions are sub–use cases that detail what happens when the main use case cannot be followed from end to end. This is very common in Web applications, and it's extremely important to address the alternative workflows because no one—and I mean no one—uses an application exactly the same way you do, or how you might have intended them to use it.

(Quick story: I once spent several days using and testing an application to see how it held up against the latest changes. I didn't come across any major problems, so I set up an account for my wife to let her try it out. The *very first thing* she did was break it. It didn't even take two minutes. The lesson to learn? No two people will use a Web application the same way, so you can't test only the *ideal* way of completing a task. You have to test *all* the ways it can be completed.)

In Step 3 of the use case above, a user could decide not to complete the form. To explain how to deal with this, I added a simple exception to the use case.

The final version looked like this:

Submit a Recommendation

Step 1.   User clicks the **Write a Recommendation** link, and a short form displays immediately beneath the button. Tech note: This form resides in a hidden DIV and loads with the rest of the page. The button toggles to read **Close** instead of **Write a Recommendation**.

Step 2.   User completes the form.

Step 3.   User clicks **OK** to submit the recommendation, and a success message displays above the form.

Step 4.   User clicks the **Close** button to close the form.

Exceptions

Step 3a. User clicks the **Close** button without completing the form. Tech note: This resembles a "cancel" action, in which input data would be stripped from the form and the form is hidden, but since the DIV is simply toggled between hide and show states, the data is retained by default and can be displayed again if the user clicks **Write a Recommendation** a second time.

"3a" indicates that the exception applies to Step 3 in the use case. It means that if the user decides not to complete the form, another workflow begins, which is detailed in Step 3a. Simple as that. Use cases can get rather lengthy, of course, when detailing complicated or large sets of interactions, but each use case often ends up very similar to this example.

Typical use cases don't go into the details of what buttons appear where or anything else that specific, but I find it incredibly useful to add these details, because it gives graphic designers and developers a more exact idea of how the interaction should look and work. It also forces me to think through whether the interaction is technically possible, and how simple or complex it will really be when it's up and running. In this use case, I was able to find a way to consolidate two buttons into a single button with two purposes. (In the real version, I also included information about the form itself—how the fields were labeled, how big they were, and all that jazz—but such details aren't important for this example.)

As you can see from the initial use case, I was making a big assumption about the interaction. I was assuming I could just throw up a simple form that would drop into place on demand and call it a day. And the developer who would eventually build the thing would have made other assumptions—for example, that the form should have two buttons: one that opens the form and one that submits the data. He would have built exactly what I said to build, *as he understood it*, and the interaction would have turned out pretty badly.

Then, I would have written up a review of the interaction, explaining to the developer that it was all wrong, and he would have had to rework his code, rather substantially, to correct the interaction. And in my review, I might have left out another detail, and thus the process could have gone on for days, adding to the developer's growing frustration, increasing my stress level, and wasting many hours of expensive and valuable programming time.

By taking 20 minutes to write an effective use case at the start, I avoided most of the pitfalls.

The rather obvious secret is this: It's far easier to change a sentence in a Word document than it is to rewrite code that runs conditional logic to perform a specific operation in an interactive system (what a mouthful!).

It takes much less time to write a use case than it does to create an interaction in HTML, with the JavaScript and CSS needed to make it all work. And more often than not, a use case is all you need to explain to another person—like a developer—how a task will be completed in an application.

Get the picture? Use cases rock.

Applying kaizen to use cases

Before we discuss the arguments against use cases, I'd like to share some quick, practical advice about how to make them as effective as possible:

Programmers often enjoy the task of "refactoring" their code to make it cleaner, run better, and contain less bugs. I'm a former programmer myself, so I may be a bit biased, but I enjoy making similar improvements to use cases (as in the example above).

Whenever I write use cases, I like to apply a little kaizen to the process. **Kaizen** is Japanese for "change for the better," or, more simply, " improvement." It was originally used as a management technique (it is credited as the reason Toyota consistently builds high-quality, long-lasting vehicles and can justify higher costs as a result), but I find kaizen can be applied to just about anything.

For every interaction I spell out with a use case, I go back over it several times, each time trying to find a way to make it smoother, faster, easier—more *obvious*. It doesn't matter whether the use case ends up changing at all. What matters is that time is spent trying to improve it. Any little detail that can be modified to improve the intuitiveness of the interaction is fantastic, but not every "improvement" is really an improvement.

For example, in the use case about submitting product recommendations, one thing I could do to make the activity easier to complete is to simply show the form by default instead of hiding it away until the user clicks the Write a Recommendation link. This translates to at least one less click for every user who decides to submit a product recommendation. Easier, no?

The downside is that the form would be displayed all the time, cluttering up the page for the 98 percent of people who will never use it. This translates to a more cluttered page every single time it's viewed. No, not easier.

However, one improvement I could make is to have the form "remember" (via a JavaScript cookie) the user's name and email address the next time she writes a recommendation, so she only has to enter the information once. This feature wouldn't be apparent the first time she used the form, but repeat submissions would enable her to complete the form more quickly.

Another improvement would be to **auto-focus** the first empty input field. If the user's name and email address are retained from previous visits, those fields will already be filled out when the user accesses the form again, so the first empty field would be the one in which she would write the actual product recommendation. If I created the form so that the cursor went immediately to that field, she could click **Write a Recommendation** and begin typing without having to click in the field first.

This would be a definite improvement. I wish I'd thought of it before I sent the use case to the developer.

Kaizen is a simple concept that can produce great results. Remembering the user's name and email address is a tiny detail, but it makes completing the form a breeze. Users may not even realize the form works this way, but as they see how easy it is to write a recommendation, they will be prone to do it more often.

Funny. That's exactly what you *want* users to do. See how well that works?

In case you missed the point: Improving usability means improving the chances users will do what you want them to do. A little kaizen can take you a long way.

The argument against use cases

Some people dispute the merits of doing anything that doesn't directly contribute to the final product. They say it's bad to spend your time on anything but code. Instead of learning about your users, design products for which *you* are the target audience. Instead of creating wireframes (which I'll talk about in Chapter 4), create a sketch and go straight to HTML.

This approach has its merits, but many of us work in environments that simply don't fit with this style of development. My job, for example, is to design interfaces for and perform heuristic evaluations on several major applications, none of which are targeted at someone like me. Different development teams are in charge of building and maintaining each one. There are far too many interfaces, interactions, task flows, and applications to deal with to go straight to code, and it would be difficult to maintain a sense of consistency between the applications without the support of a large design team.

Again, use whatever design and development process you like, but give use cases a whirl before writing them off. You'll likely find they're a fast, cheap, and easy way to get all those fuzzy ideas on paper and start seeing the possibilities and problems.

My advice

My advice is this: Learn as much as you can about users in general—not necessarily the user base specific to your applications—so you know how they use Web-based products, but then focus on the activity your application is meant to support and design for that.

To design anything well for the Web, you have to know how people work with it, but as long as you have an ongoing, general understanding of users, designing for the activity enables you to develop and maintain a vision for your product and avoid bending to the whims of users. (More about this in the next chapter.)

If understanding the activity your application supports means talking to people about the activity and how they perform it, the approaches outlined in this chapter will help you do that. So, in addition to gaining a general understanding of Web users, you can gain an understanding of any activity that can be supported by a well-designed Web application. Armed with this knowledge, you're well on your way to designing the obvious. The rest of the work is figuring out how you implement interfaces that support the qualities of great Web-based software, and I'll spend the rest of this book talking about how to bring those details to life.

3

Build Only What Is Absolutely Necessary

▶ **Think Different**

▶ **Drop Nice-to-Have Features**

When applications evolve based on the demands of users, they tend to take a bad turn.

Features used by only 10 percent of users, or used only 10 percent of the time, are added and get in the way of the remaining 90 percent of features. They clutter an otherwise clean interface. They interfere with the features used most often.

And when "featuritis" takes over, you quickly find yourself permanently providing tech support for things that shouldn't be in the tool to begin with, fixing more bugs, writing more help material, and neglecting other, more important features. And while this may sound like a lot of fun to certain (slightly crazy) programmers, it's clearly the wrong approach.

The focus should not be on features, the focus should be on *focus.* An obvious application is a focused application. It's easy to explain to other people. It makes sense to those using it because the purpose of the tool is self-evident, and nothing in it strays from that purpose. Every feature supports the single activity the application is designed to support.

More features, more frustration

A user's frustration level does not usually correspond directly to the number of difficult features in an application. Frustration can actually increase exponentially. For every additional feature, there is more to learn, more to tweak and configure, more to customize, more to read about in the help documentation, and *more that can go wrong.*

For you, it's one more feature. For users, it's one more thing that adds to the already long list of frustrating things to deal with while using a computer. It's not just your application—it's everything else, too.

It's the operating system, which hides files away in obscure file-system directories and is constantly popping up little dialog boxes and error messages that you are forced to address so you can get on with your real work.

It's the browser, which has no graceful way of indicating whether or not the link you just clicked is going to show you what you want to see.

It's the email client, which offers no insights into how long it will take for the message you just wrote, with the rather large photo of your cat, to be sent to your grandmother.

Users contend with all these things and more during the same stretch of time they try to deal with your Web application. And the frustrations add up quickly.

I know, I know—none of these things bother you at all. They don't really bother me either. But that's a sad fact. It means we've become desensitized to things that are otherwise maddening. It means we've gone numb.

In short, we've become "computer-savvy."

So what's a geek to do?

You have to have killer features or your application won't be able to stand up to its competitors. You have to keep adding things to new versions or no one will purchase upgrades (assuming your Web application requires periodic upgrades). And you have to match the competition one-for-one so no one will ever say your application is light where the other guy's is robust.

To paraphrase Alan Cooper, however, trying to match competing products feature for feature is like running through a battleground under cover fire. You can run all you want, but you have to keep shooting to get anywhere. Dishing out cover fire keeps you alive for a few minutes at a time. Long enough to hide. Companies that fight all the time to stay ahead fall into the endless cycle of trying to outdo the enemy (if the enemy has a big gun, you need a bigger gun). This goes on and on until someone falls. It's not a fun way to do things. It's a method that works only as long as the people fighting the battle continue to come up with bigger guns. They spend all their time spraying out cover fire while they run three feet to the next safe position.

Many companies live and die this way. To get into the fight, you have to stock up on venture capital, go into major debt, hire a bunch of rock star developers, go straight to code because there's no time to plan or design anything, and rush, rush, rush to market with a 27-page list of features. And if the enemy starts to catch up, you have to add more features, call the next version "the most robust release ever," and try to maintain your market share. Until, of course, the enemy puts out a new version with even *more* features.

It's exhausting.

It's also exhausting for users. The more features you offer, the more the user has to learn. The more options you provide, the more users have to do to get anything done. The more you allow customization, the more users have to fidget and tweak and manipulate your application. They spend more time configuring the tool than using it. As a result of fighting the fight, complicated applications often end up much less usable than one would hope.

To stay alive, you eventually have to get out of the line of fire. It's the only real option.

▶ Think Different

Firewheel Design (www.firewheeldesign.com) got out of the line of fire by creating Blinksale (www.blinksale.com), a Web-based invoicing system. The simple application contains only the features that are absolutely necessary for the largest percentage of its users to successfully create, submit, and track invoices.

Firewheel's decision to minimize Blinksale's feature list might look like a mistake because it seems as if it won't be able to compete in the rat race with the big boys of invoicing systems. But Firewheel did something the big boys haven't done. It got out of the line of fire by creating something that makes it stand out from all the rest.

Blinksale is aimed at contractors who don't need to do anything fancy with their invoices. Many people who need to submit and track invoices need only a few basic tools. These include a way to create the invoice, submit it, mark it as closed when payment is received, and perhaps send a receipt confirmation to the client. When the folks at Firewheel Design set out to create Blinksale, they realized they could keep it simple and satisfy the vast majority of user needs. They may have even realized that making it more complicated would decrease their chances of satisfying user needs. So they designed an application that does one thing, and does it very well: It gives people a fast and effective way to create, submit, and track invoices.

(See how easy it is to explain? That's a good sign.)

The system can be used by plenty of people besides contractors because it's so stripped down, a trained monkey could use it (if the trained monkey did, say, carpentry work on the side). The application contains just a few key features.

The dashboard and New Invoice screen

When you log in, Blinksale shows you a summary of your recent activity (open invoices, past-due invoices, and so on) so you get a quick, at-a-glance, dashboard-style view of the state of your invoices. It offers three easy-to-spot buttons, each of which is used to create one of three invoice types.

You simply choose the client the invoice is for, or create a new one (right there, on the same page) and hop over to the New Invoice page. This page looks like a real invoice, so you maintain context the whole time you're creating it. All the fields you need to complete are displayed as form elements so you can simply edit the invoice onscreen and click the big <u>Save Invoice</u> button.

Blinksale's main invoice-editing screen is easy to use.

When you're done, you see the final version of the invoice and a few new buttons, which let you send the invoice, edit it, or delete it. One click of the

<u>Send Invoice</u> button produces an in-line form on which you checkmark all the people in the client company to whom you want to send the invoice and write an optional message.

The finished invoice

The invoice itself is an HTML-formatted email that looks great right out of the box (well, the browser), and you don't have to configure anything at all to send off a professional invoice to a client in five minutes or less.

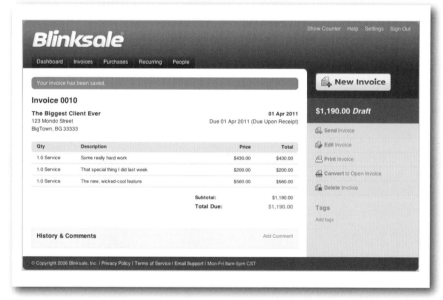

Blinksale generates easy-to-read invoices and lets you email them to your clients in a click.

Simple as that.

Goodies for experts

The more adept Blinksale users out there have the option to subscribe to their invoices using the iCalendar format, which means Mac users can track invoices using Mac OS X's built-in calendar application, iCal. You can also export the invoice data as an XML file or Excel spreadsheet, so if you decide to cancel your Blinksale account, you can retain all your data.

As for settings, Blinksale has a few basic templates from which to choose how you want your invoices to look. You can also send reminders to clients about late payments and create thank-you messages to send to clients who pay their bills on time.

The whole application takes about 30 minutes to learn inside and out, and just about pays for itself every time you create an invoice (at the time of this writing, Blinksale ran $6 per month for up to 20 invoices, with plans of up to $29 per month for 500 invoices).

Firewheel built only what was absolutely necessary for most people to successfully handle the activity of invoicing clients. There are no obscure configuration options, no redundant functionality (there's exactly one way to complete each task in the tool, which makes it easy to learn), and no fancy interface widgets to figure out. It just does exactly what it should, and it does it within a simple, clean interface that somehow makes invoices seem friendly, like someone you'd want to take to lunch. (We'll talk more about software personality in Chapter 9.)

The result

Josh Williams, one of the creators of Blinksale, is justifiably proud of how things turned out. He recently told me:

> *As a small design company we did our fair share of client billing. Unfortunately we've always been less than enamored with the off-the-shelf invoicing and billing software that is available at your local office supply store. After a few years of frustration we set out to build our own Web-based invoicing service. Goal number one was ease of use. Goal number two was keeping our cost of design and development of the service low. Remarkably, these two goals often go hand in hand.*

Firewheel could have designed Blinksale to be chock-full of features that did everything from integrate with Intuit QuickBooks in 12 easy steps to prepare tax information and let you export it to Intuit TurboTax at the end of the year. They could have built a product that rivaled its competition feature for feature. They didn't. They built the 20 percent people actually need. Nothing more. Nothing less.

And while there are a few extra gadgets thrown in for more computer-savvy users, Blinksale does a great job of keeping things simple and focused. If all you want to do is create an invoice and send it off to a client—the single task most people will spend most of their time completing in Blinksale—you can do it in just a few minutes and be on your merry way.

▶ Drop Nice-to-Have Features

Almost every application I've ever used has contained at least a few features that were probably first described in a statement that started with "Something that would be really nice to have is *<insert description here>.*" But most of these things are exactly what clutter up interfaces all over the Web, and it's our job to fend these things off with a big stick. They need to be removed from your next application before it's even built. An obvious interface is one that is focused on what's most important and leaves out the things that are simply "nice to have."

In its book *Getting Real,* 37signals has this to say about focusing on only the important features:

> *Stick to what's truly essential. Good ideas can be tabled.* **Take whatever you think your product should be and cut it in half.** *Pare features down until you're left with only the most essential ones. Then do it again.*

The statement is similar to something Steve Krug said in his book *Don't Make Me Think,* one of the greatest books out there on Web usability. It's Krug's Third Law of Usability:

> *Get rid of half the words on each page, then get rid of half of what's left.*

And Krug's law can be traced back to William Strunk and E. B. White's *The Elements of Style:*

> *Vigorous writing is concise. A sentence should contain no unnecessary words, a paragraph no unnecessary sentences, for the same reason that a drawing should have no unnecessary lines and a machine no unnecessary parts.*

Say it again, brother.

All these people are in the business of simplicity. Simplicity makes the point clear. It lets messages stand out. It offers communication that cuts through the noise.

The Unnecessary Test

To create applications that cut through the noise, you have to be willing to slice your application's feature list down to its bare bones, and you have to recognize what's most important.

With that in mind, try the following exercise, which I call the Unnecessary Test:

Open a Web application you've worked on recently and find a feature you thought was really important a long time ago, perhaps before you started building the application.

Ask yourself the following question:

Does this feature contribute directly to the user's ability to complete a task that is vital to the activity this application is meant to support?

If you answered no to this question, the feature can be deemed unnecessary. You've found yourself a likely candidate for the cutting room floor.

If, on the other hand, you answered yes, either you're looking at a rock star feature or you're not looking hard enough at the feature to be objective. Try your best to detach yourself from all the work you did and ask the question from a more objective point of view.

Regardless of your answer, it's likely there are several features in your application that could be scrapped, so you should take the time to go through every feature and run each one through the Unnecessary Test.

When you're done with the testing, close the application and ask yourself three more questions.

1. What is the activity my application is meant to support?

2. If this application didn't exist, and I needed to perform the same activity this application is meant to support, and the world was perfect, and I could wave a magic wand to create an application that helped me complete this activity—the core activity—with the greatest of ease, what would the application do? (Hint: You should limit this answer to three or four very big-picture statements that relate to the principle goal of the activity.)

3. How long would it take to rebuild my application to make it do that?

Sorry—that last question is a joke (sort of). After all, you're likely to have answered one of the first two questions in a way that prevents you from having to admit you were wrong. I know—I've done this myself. It's difficult to admit your application may not be living up to its promise.

If this is true, have someone else answer the same set of questions and see if the answers come out differently. Even better, ask one of your users.

I'm not suggesting you start ripping functionality out of an existing application. Doing this could have the rather negative side effect of making some of your users extremely upset. To the people using the more obscure features, removing them would be a huge mistake. I'm only suggesting you learn from what you've already done so you can create more focused applications in the future.

The 60-Second Deadline

Here's another quick way to learn to effectively aim low and keep your application focused on the 20 percent that matters. Pretend I'm your boss. I walk into your office and very matter-of-factly state, "The project time line has been cut in half. We have about 60 seconds to decide what to keep and what to throw away before we meet with the client in the conference room."

How do you respond to this statement?

Whatever you do, don't impulsively offer up the theoretical answer—the one where you say how much you'd love the low-carb sandwich.

Figure out the real answer.

Grab a notepad and a pen, write down the list of features you have planned for an upcoming application, and see what you can cut in 60 seconds. Draw a line through each feature you can cut without completely destroying the application.

The goal is to leave yourself only with what is most essential for the application to serve its purpose.

Bells? Gone.

Whistles? Gone.

Show me only the pieces you absolutely have to keep for the tool to do its job.

When you're done, cut one more feature, just for good measure. Cut the one you're holding onto only because it's really cool. C'mon, I know there's at least one on your original list. Draw a line though it.

Your 60 seconds are up. Good job.

Now, take out a second sheet of paper and write a new list that shows only what you have left, just so you can see it sitting there all nice and clean. Looks much better, doesn't it? I know, it probably hurts a bit to have lost so much stuff, but I bet your application is now easier to explain.

Finally, take out another sheet of paper and write down the list of things you drew a line through earlier. Title this page "Nice-to-Have Features," stick it in your filing cabinet, and forget about it. We'll look at it again later.

The first time you do this, it can be quite revealing. You may find you've been wasting a lot of your time and energy on things that don't really contribute to the application in any meaningful way. Of course, this may be a bit unsettling, but hey, knowing is half the battle. Next time around, you can use the Unnecessary Test and the 60-Second Deadline exercise before you start coding, to see what really needs to be built—and you can spend all your time working to make those things as good as they can be.

And since building what's most important takes much less time than building what's not important, you can get more sleep, take more vacations, get more weekends off, and live a happier, healthier life.

Or you could do what I do and use all that saved time to build more applications. I know that's what you *really* want to do.

Less is more

Regardless of how you do it, the ultimate goal is to determine what's most important to the application by whittling your list of features down to about 20 percent of what was built or what you were planning to build. Yes, some of the remaining 80 percent of your features may be useful somehow, to someone, some of the time, but they are most likely useless to 80 percent of your users, 80 percent of the time. And you probably spent 80 percent of your development time building things that aren't essential to the application.

This is because the 80-20 rule has made its way into the world of Web-based software.

Known formally as the Pareto principle (named for Vilfredo Pareto), the 80-20 rule was originally suggested to indicate that 80 percent of consequences are the result of 20 percent of causes.

In terms of good, clean Web application design, it means that 80 percent of an application's usefulness comes from 20 percent of its features. It also works the other way around, to illustrate that 20 percent of the development work produces 80 percent of an application. The other 80 percent of the work is needed to satisfy only 20 percent of users.

To create more focused applications, stick to building the 20 percent of fea-tures that are essential, and you'll take care of 80 percent of the user's needs. Let your competitors worry about the rest. While they're floundering around trying to one-up you by fleshing out the other 80 percent of the application, you could be taking 80 percent more vacations and enjoying 80 percent of the market share.

Less is more. Aim low.

Interface Surgery

A Web-based job application form I saw once was composed of two windows. One window got the user through the first few screens of the process, and then launched a second window to complete the bulk of the application. The first window was connected to the user's log-in session, which was timed, and was designed to log out the user automatically if the system remained inactive for 20 minutes. The second window was not tied to the session. So, when a user tried to complete the job application in the second window, the part of the process that took the longest amount of time, the system invari-ably logged the user out after 20 minutes, rudely doing so without any noti-fication whatsoever.

The company's solution was to add a bit of text in the original window warn-ing users that they would be logged out after 20 minutes—a weak attempt to get those pesky users to stop complaining. This was a band-aid. It did not solve the problem, it just told people what to expect. Users would still have to com-plete the job application in 20 minutes or less. The company was essentially saying, "Sure, we've created a terrible system that will likely terminate your session before you can complete your job application, but hey, we're warning you before you start, so it's OK!"

I don't like band-aids.

Instead of putting band-aids on problems, I perform surgery on them. Inter-face Surgery.

In this first installment of Interface Surgery, we'll cut out a bunch of unnecessary features from a fictitious Web-based email application being designed for a fictitious Web-hosting company. Instead of finding ways to make a ton of unnecessary gadgets easier to present and use, we're going to rip them out and leave only what's absolutely essential for the application to do its job.

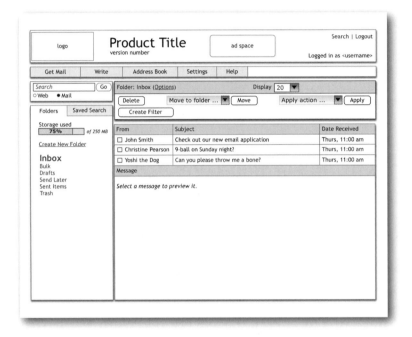

This application has a ton of features. In addition to being able to simply check your email, you can search the Web, see how much storage space you've used, make sure you're logged in using a particular user name, reuse saved searches, apply actions (such as set up an automatic response email), move email to other folders you create yourself, configure options for the Inbox (such as font settings), and even change how many messages should be displayed in the list before having to switch to a new page.

Some of these things are necessary, some are not.

To get started, let's strip out the part of the Search feature that lets users search the Web. There are plenty of other ways to search the Web, and many modern browsers feature a built-in search bar, making Web search accessible 100 percent of the time the user has the browser open. There's no need to replicate what's already ubiquitous. And since we're leaving only the option to search mail, we can remove the two radio buttons and shrink down the space this piece takes up.

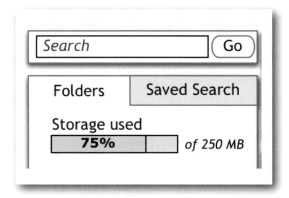

Let's also get rid of the ability to save searches. It's more difficult to save a search, find it again later, and rerun it than it is to simply reenter a few keywords. This might be nice for some users, but it's not going to seriously benefit *most users, most of the time.* And since we're getting rid of it, we can lose the tabbed interface used to display it. Since the Folders view is now the only option, it no longer needs a label or a tab.

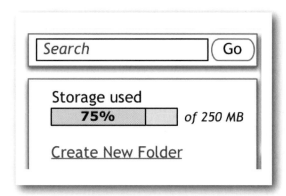

Next, let's get rid of the percentage indicator that tells users how much storage space has been used up. If we decide this is essential later, we can move it into the Settings screen. There's no reason to give it a permanent position in the main interface.

Next, let's get rid of the text that indicates which user is currently logged in. This is unnecessary most of the time, because most users will only ever have a single account, and since they have to manually log themselves in before they can see this screen, it's pointless to show them something they already know.

Also, let's kill the option to change how many messages display in the list at once. This can certainly be retained as a feature, but it's not the kind of thing users are going to use every day, so we can move it to the Settings screen.

And since a Search bar is provided in the left-hand sidebar, we can remove the Search link from the top of the page.

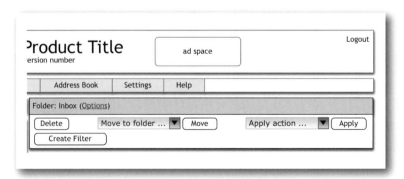

Showing a title bar for which folder is currently being displayed is redundant, because the label for the folder in the sidebar is made larger and bold when that folder is displayed. And if we remove the Folder title bar, we can free up some vertical space for more important content—like *mail*.

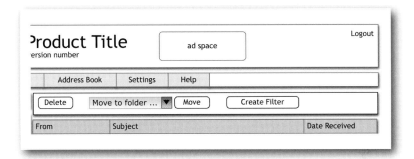

When an email is being displayed, another small bar appears above the email offering **Reply**, **Reply All**, **Forward**, and **Delete** functions, as well as a way to mark an email as junk.

But there's already a **Delete** button in the bar above the message list. If we remove it and tidy things up a bit, we can consolidate the bar and unify the message options into a single interface element, which means less code, less interface, and less confusion.

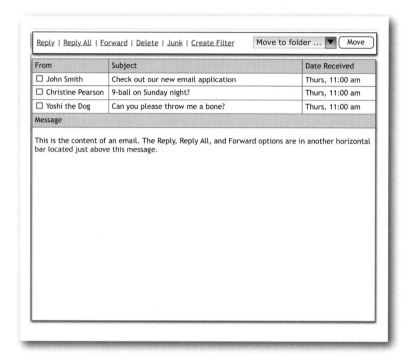

Finally, let's add some logic to the application and have it disable the **Reply**, **Reply All**, and **Forward** links if more than one message is selected at a time. **Delete**, **Junk**, and **Create Filter** can all be applied to multiple messages, so we'll leave those active. In doing this, we make the message options more functional while still taking up less space.

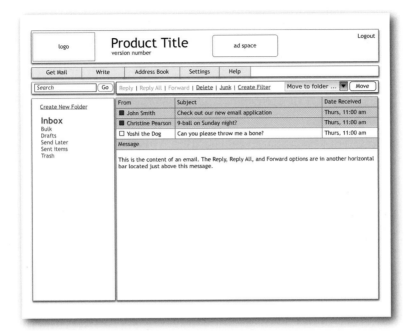

Ahh, that's much better. We stripped out a few features, removed a few interface elements, cleaned things up, and came out with an application interface that is easier to understand at a quick glance and easier to use on a daily basis.

We'll perform interface surgery throughout this book as a way of improving applications one step at a time.

Reevaluate nice-to-have features later

So, when is it time to take the list of nice-to-have features back out of the filing cabinet?

The simple answer is this: not one second before your application has been released.

Once your application is out there, being used by real users, and you've given it some time to stabilize by fixing a lot of the immediate bugs that have inevitably come up since the release, then it's time to review the list of nice-to-haves. It's also time for a good laugh.

What usually happens is that users start to speak up about what they wish your application did, things that bother them, and so on, and no one ever mentions the items on your list of nice-to-haves. Users very quickly form different perspectives on your application than you may have ever had, and since none of them use the application exactly the way you thought they would, the complaints and wish lists that emerge are usually different than what you thought was important.

If this is the case for you, feel free to put that list of nice-to-haves into the *other* filing cabinet—the one shaped like a trash can—and call it a day. The things we often think are so important at the beginning of a project usually prove to be about as useful as adding another color to a logo. And more often than not, adding them way back when would have meant putting the rock star features at risk by making them harder to find, harder to configure, *harder to use.*

Let them speak

Once your application is being used out in the wild and you want to hear all the little screaming voices of your users, you need to give them a way to talk to you. Larger companies typically offer customer-support avenues like email addresses or phone numbers so users can ask questions when they get stuck or complain when they're upset. But there are some lessons to be learned from the world of marketing that might be more valuable.

Seth Godin, author of many best-selling books on the subject of marketing, including *The Big Red Fez,* is a major advocate of *viral marketing* on the Web. This basically means providing a way for users to talk about your product and then getting out of the way so they can talk freely. Not only is this a great marketing tool—you're creating a way for your customers to recommend your products to other people—but it also provides great insight into what problems customers are having and what they'd like to change or add to the product so you can keep those things on your radar. Something as simple as setting up a forum on your site and directing people there from your Support page can dramatically lower your customer-support costs (a forum costs extremely little to maintain), while greatly increasing the amount of information you get from customers.

Note, however, that you will probably not like everything that gets posted. Invariably, there will be some dissatisfied and possibly rude users who do nothing but scream about your "horrible" application, saying nothing constructive, but you have to let this happen. If you moderate user comments to filter out the negative, you'll defeat the purpose of the forum, which is to hear the complaints. The goal is to feel the pain.

When you allow your users to speak up, you'll quickly come up with a whole new list of nice-to-haves. Put those in the filing cabinet as well.

Avoid bending to users' whims if the high-demand features don't fit into your grand vision for the application. You might try pooling a few internal beta users together and have them try out a prototype of the proposed functionality to see how it really works before unleashing it on all your customers. There's no shame in pulling the feature back out if it just doesn't work. Better now than later.

Focus only on the features that are in the most demand, the ones that are most important.

4

Support the User's Mental Model

- ▶ Design for Mental Models
- ▶ Eliminate Implementation Models
- ▶ Prototype the Design
- ▶ Test It Out

When we consider how to organize papers, we may think of filing cabinets. We fill filing cabinets with hanging folders, and fill those with manila folders, each with its own stack of files. We use labeling systems to help us remember what each folder contains.

In modern operating systems, we can glance around a virtual desktop full of folders (represented by icons), spot the one we need, open it up, and scan its contents to find the file we need.

In reality, though, computers use addresses to tell them where each specific bit and byte is stored. The addresses on the hard disk don't need to correspond to a filing system—in fact, two files stored in the same folder do not necessarily exist in consecutive spaces on the hard drive.

As another example, when we think about throwing something away, we usually think of trash cans. Trash cans sit in every room in our houses and offices, and do nothing but give us a place to toss items we no longer need.

Today, instead of entering obscure terminology into a command-line tool to delete a file—which is how it used to be done—we throw it away. We drag a file icon to another icon shaped like a trash can or recycling bin. The visual metaphor has replaced the typed command, and deleting files has come to mean throwing them away.

Much like throwing something away in real life, the trash metaphor used by Mac OS X lets us visualize the removal of an item in a way that supports our mental model.

In actuality, the metaphor of throwing something away bears no resemblance to deleting a file from a computer. But which makes more sense to you? The act of throwing a file in the trash can, or deleting an address from the hard drive's index so the storage space can be overwritten the next time the computer needs to save to the hard drive?

The useful, concrete mental metaphor has effectively replaced the reality of what occurs—and no one cares! The metaphor works, and is much simpler than the reality.

In both of these cases, users have been given visual metaphors that adhere more closely to our knowledge of the world outside of our computers. Trash cans are used for trash, and filing cabinets are used for organizing files. This is how we do things in real life, and now this is (more or less) how we do things on a computer. What we believe about what happens has nothing to do with the reality of what happens on the computer. But we rely on our real-world experiences to help us assimilate and understand.

Understanding mental models

A **mental model**, in other words, is what we believe to be true, generally based on our experiences, and how we assimilate new things into our existing knowledge. It doesn't have to be the truth, and it usually isn't. It just has to settle in our heads well enough to let us sleep at night. It has to help us understand how to *use* a computer and understand what it *is*, but not necessarily what it really does.

For users to feel good about an application, they need to feel as if they understand it. Making it as simple as possible for them to understand—even if that simple understanding is completely inaccurate—is designing the obvious. Of course, the inaccurate understanding has to be useful as a way of thinking and simplifying, but as long as that's true, the design has a better chance of succeeding.

In other words, it's OK if the user is completely wrong in her perception of what is happening as long as her sense of understanding makes her feel good and competent, and she can accomplish her goals with her understanding, regardless of how faulty it might be.

An **implementation model**, on the other hand, is something that has been designed, usually by not being "designed" at all, to reflect the underlying details of a system. Implementation models have no regard for a system's users. They aim, usually, to please the geeks that create them.

That old DOS prompt, which required us to understand how to forcibly remove a file from the dark shadows of the hard drive index, is an example of an implementation model. We were expected to know how the hard drive works, how to remove an item from it, and so on. Now, we just throw the darn thing away.

In Web applications, many implementation-model designs appear even when there are far better ways to represent the functionality the interface elements are intended to handle. This chapter is about how to avoid implementation models and design interfaces that make sense to users without forcing them to understand the underlying technologies.

▶ Design for Mental Models

When a Web application uses implementation models to represent its functionality, a few common trends emerge.

First, error messages tend to read like bug reports written specifically for the developers who wrote them. Programmers often need to add code to applications during development that helps them debug issues as they arise, and the error messages are written in words that help the developers narrow down the issue. Before the application is released, this is fine, but these cryptic messages often live on into released applications and mystify users to no end. These messages reveal the system from the developer's perspective instead of revealing the system's benefits by improving a user's understanding.

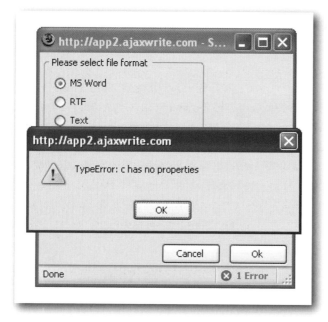

This error message is not only meaningless to users, it interferes with their ability to learn how the application works and their ability to be productive.

Second, interfaces often become overly complicated. Because programmers enjoy exposing every option and setting a system could possibly contain, interfaces offer up buttons, configurations, settings, dialog boxes, panels, and menus that do everything but wash the dishes.

Instead of focusing on focus, implementation-model designs focus on covering all the bases. They sacrifice ease of use in favor of the fine level of control a system is capable of allowing.

Programmers, who are usually the first to admit they are more computer-savvy than the rest of the world, often want incredible amounts of control over the applications they work with, so they surface everything they can in the applications they build, regardless of how difficult it makes a tool to learn for someone who lacks the experience of a programmer. Their users typically don't want this fine level of control. They want to understand how to get their work done and go home to their kids and spouses and dogs.

Just yesterday, I was shown a design for a blog template that featured a small section in the sidebar used to show a list of keywords associated with the post currently being viewed. The list could be shown in two ways. One way was as a **tag cloud**, which uses larger fonts to display more relevant keywords and smaller fonts to represent less relevant keywords. The other way was as a plain list where each item used the same font and font size. Two buttons, labeled Cloud and List, were offered so users could switch between the tag-cloud view and the list view. When I asked why the buttons were there, the designer told me a developer had said something like, "It would be nice if users had a choice to display the list both ways."

I understand where the developer was coming from. Developers like to cover their bases and offer everything they can. If it's *possible* to show the list in two ways, we think the choice *should* be offered. But most users viewing this particular page online will not know what a tag cloud is, and those who do will likely not want to switch between the two views. Providing them the choice is pointless. Users who see a tag cloud and understand it will benefit from being able to quickly discern between the relevancy of the various keywords, and those who don't get it will still see a simple list of keywords. No harm, no foul.

But when presented with the option to switch between the two views, every user without preexisting knowledge of a tag cloud would have to try to figure out what was meant by the two buttons. Users would be forced to learn something they don't need to know in order to become comfortable with the page. The choice doesn't help anyone, and actually distracts users from achieving a basic understanding of the page's functionality. The implementation-model design would have impeded a user's chances of successfully using the page.

Thankfully, the designer decided to scrap the two buttons and just show the tag cloud.

A third trend that results from the use of implementation-model designs is that tasks often become cumbersome and frustrating because the system needs all sorts of particular bits of information to complete an operation, and it forces you to tweak and guide it at every step so it can complete the operation in the exact way you tell it. It doesn't help you form a simple understanding of how to make it work, it forces you to understand it so it can get what *it* needs. To this end, it pokes and prods at you until it gets everything out of you it can.

This approach manifests itself as labels that mean nothing to someone who doesn't know how the system works, positioned next to pieces of functionality that should never have been surfaced in the first place. Like a button labeled **Cloud**.

This behavior is, well, rude. It's about making users do everything they can to make the system happy and not doing what makes *users* happy. Applications like this try hard to be all things to all people, and end up failing to be anything great to anyone. Yes, these applications can still succeed, but it is often because of other factors, such as the lack of any other application in the market that fulfills a similar purpose. This sad fact doesn't make it OK for applications to be rude, but they end up that way far too often because the mighty implementation model rears its ugly head.

When applications work well, however, and allow users to easily form their own, more comforting mental models, everybody wins.

Making metaphors that work

Backpack (www.backpackit.com), created by 37signals (www.37signals.com), is a wonderful and very simple tool for managing small projects and chunks of information. Backpack allows you to create Web pages you can fill up with . . . stuff. You know, like you can fill up a backpack.

This sample page from Backpack shows to-do list items, notes, files, and images all being managed in a single page.

In Backpack, you simply click a button to create a page, name it, and then start filling it up with anything you need to get yourself organized. Notes, images, files, and to-do lists can all be kept in a single page.

Prior to Backpack, whenever I sank my teeth into some new research or small project, I would invariably start compiling information. I'd create a folder on my desktop and start throwing files into it. I'd create a bookmarks folder in my browser and start adding bookmarks to it. I'd collect images. I'd write lists. I'd write more notes. I'd go crazy with disorganization.

With Backpack, however, I can keep all that information in one place, just as if I were a student throwing books, homework, notes, and perhaps even my lunch into my backpack. Instead of the implementation model of the operating system, which says that bookmarks, files, to-do lists, and images are all different things that are stored in different software applications and folders, Backpack supports my mental model of how information like this is organized in real life. My real-world backpack lets me keep it all in one place. Now, my Web-based backpack does as well.

At first, I understood Backpack's purpose and saw definite potential in it, but I wasn't sure it would be really useful for me. But I signed up for the free account and decided to give it a whirl to organize all the notes and such I needed to write an article I was working on that week.

By the next day, I was completely sold, and upgraded to a paying account. Backpack let me get organized in a way that allowed me to maintain structure and relationships between formerly disparate bits of data and see it as a single collection that has meaning and context for me. Information and ideas tend to come in sporadic waves, and Backpack lets me work within this free-flowing state, without forcing me to use phrases like "maintain structure and relationships between formerly disparate bits of data." It lets me keep my own model of how all these bits of data go together, where I used to be stuck with the operating system's methods of organization.

When I asked Jason Fried, the fearless leader of 37signals, about the inspiration for Backpack, he said:

> *Like every product we build, the motivation is to scratch our own itch. We needed Backpack to "keep life's loose ends together" so we built Backpack. Our experience with organizational software was that it was too complex.*

It asked you too many questions and imposed too much structure. The truth is that information comes in chaotic streams and you just need a place to capture it all. You can organize it later, but if you don't get it out of your head and into a central location you'll forget about it. So Backpack was designed to bring all this loose information together in one central location. Then you can use Backpack's simple to-do list, notes, text, image, files, and reminder tools to shape it into something that makes more sense to you.

Rolling over the page title displays an Edit link. Clicking it converts the page title into an editable text field, in which you can simply type a new page title. Then you just click another button to save it.

Another exciting part about Backpack is that everything on the page can be edited *right in the page*. Creating a new Note, for example, drops a text field into the page so you can just start typing. Creating a to-do list is as simple as clicking one button to create the list and typing the first item into another editable text field. Upon saving the to-do item, it converts to a check box so you can check off your to-do item later on. Adding files is a small matter of browsing to a file and uploading it.

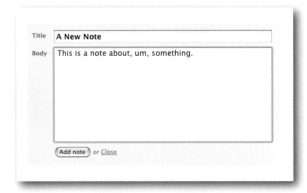

The fields you need to add a new note are dropped right into the page so you can create it without leaving the page.

You never have to wait for a new page to reload, never have to remember which link takes you to which page, never have to remember how to perform a task.

Backpack immediately became invaluable because it lets me get on with doing whatever I need to do and stays out of my way. I never see error messages while using the application, and it doesn't expect me to learn anything remarkable about its inner workings to understand how to use it. There are exactly zero hoops through which to jump.

Are you sure?

The only implementation-model piece of design I've seen while using Backpack is the JavaScript alert message that pops open when I attempt to delete something from a Backpack page. It asks, simply, "Are you sure?"

While the message is a pretty standard confirmation message—which we're all used to seeing—it's a sign of the underlying system. It's a big ol' banner that says "I don't have an undo feature and the only way I can deal with you deleting an object from your page is to interrupt your workflow with this message to make sure you know what you're doing."

Yes, yes, I'm sure. Oh, wait. What did that message say? I clicked OK out of habit and didn't even bother looking at it.

After all, in real life (which is where my mental model of deleting comes from) I can always take something out of the trash. And my trash can does not ask me if I'm sure I want to put something in it.

If it were up to me, then, I'd design an undo function for the application and get rid of the confirmation message. There's no reason not to let the user throw stuff away without confirming his or her actions, so offer an undo function— maybe a simple text link that appears in the page whenever the user performs an action that can't be undone some other way. This text link could remain available until the user performed a different action, at which point the link would change to enable an undo of the more recent action. The ability to undo the action would remain available for more time than the Java Script alert message, and it wouldn't get in the user's way when he was trying to work. Two benefits in one. It would not only hide the system from users, it would further support their mental models of how things are thrown away.

Overall, however, Backpack does a fantastic job of helping me understand its purpose. In addition to letting me do exactly what I want with it, it's aptly named. Just like a backpack in my real life, Backpack is the place I throw all my stuff so I don't need to keep it in my head. I use Backpack at work to jot down interface ideas, and at home to organize articles I'm working on and plans for personal projects. And since it's Web based, I can bring it with me wherever I go. Just like a backpack. It's quite effective at supporting my mental model of the concept of organization.

With the one exception of the JavaScript confirmation message, Backpack never reveals to me how it works or bothers me to confirm every little decision. It just works. For that, I thank 37signals. Every day.

When was the last time someone thanked you for creating such a great application?

Interface Surgery: Converting an implementation-model design into a mental-model design

One of the peskiest implementation-model widgets on the Web is the tree view interaction. Tree views are a shining example of a graphical user interface element that reflects the system's underlying structure without regard to users. In this second installment of Interface Surgery, we'll take a look at converting this implementation-model widget into a mental-model widget.

The tree view is used to display the hierarchical structure of a set of folders in a way that clearly represents the hierarchy used to create the set. And it does a great job of this. It's very easy to see from the figure below that the tree illustrates an outline view, like an outline you might create for a term paper. You see the root folder, folders nested within it, a small plus-minus icon next to each folder used to expand or collapse the folders, and you may even understand that each folder is clickable. But people don't understand tree views as much as we'd like to believe.

Behold the tree view interface, in all its glory.

I know, I know—right now you're saying, "Anyone who uses Windows knows about the tree view, because it's used in Windows Explorer." But most people don't use it because it's not the default view in Windows Explorer. The default view is a list of files and/or folders with a panel on the left that lets you perform certain actions on those files, like burn them to CD. And most people don't change the defaults because they either don't know they can, don't know how, or don't know why it would matter.

The bigger problem, however, is that the only people who really understand deep, hierarchical structures like those represented by tree views are IT people. People like us. People who use Windows Explorer all the time and understand that a Web site is often comprised of a set of nested folders, each targeted individually within the code so everything on the site displays correctly. People who understand how the file system is organized.

Regardless, developers often try to move this paradigm online, believing users will understand it. In most cases, however, they won't.

Even Microsoft concurs with this view. In its own MSDN Library (**msdn.microsoft.com/library/**) it says, "Advanced users are more proficient at using trees. If your application is aimed at novice users, avoid using tree views."

Many people outside of our world just dump everything into the My Documents folder and struggle to find files later on. And this, remarkably, works pretty well, because Windows defaults to the My Documents folder in File Open and Save As dialog boxes when it hasn't been told to point elsewhere.

In addition to the difficulty of understanding the design of tree views, these painful little widgets also tend to include a ridiculous amount of functionality. When you click on the small plus-minus icon, the nested folders either display or are hidden, respectively. When you click on a folder name, the contents of the folder are revealed in a separate panel. But the plus-minus icon doesn't do the same thing. All that does is expand or collapse the view of nested folders. It doesn't show you files. So you can expand a folder and not see its contained files, or you can click on a folder label to see its contained files without expanding the view to see its nested folders. What you can't do, however, in some tree view implementations, is click once to expand the view and see contained files at the same time.

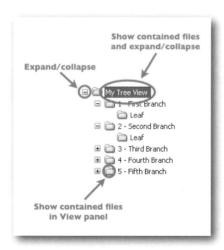

Each part of a tree does something different, and many implementations of tree view interfaces behave differently than the others. This is an example of a typical implementation.

So, in addition to the rather bizarre rules you must follow to work with a tree view, you also have to keep track of all the different versions of tree views you come across, because many of them operate differently from the others.

And if that's not enough—and maybe I'm nitpicking here—the plus-minus icon is usually very small, making it fairly difficult to roll over with a mouse so it can be clicked. It doesn't exactly scream, "Hey! I'm a button!"

All in all, it's a confusing piece of wizardry that only a geek could love. (Though I'm a geek, and I don't love it one bit.)

The myriad ways you can interact with a tree view control are all made possible by a system that does way more than it should. Developers who build these controls see all the possible ways a user can interact with the tree view, and insist on making each one an option. More options are not what's needed here. What's needed is a simpler control that provides the same functionality in a way that's easier to understand.

To get a new perspective, consider this:

Tree-view controls are used as menus. Nothing more. Nothing less. People use them to make *selections* until they find the files or data objects they're looking for. A tree view is a selection control.

With this in mind, we could just redesign tree views as menus with nested submenus, right? Well, sure, if we wanted to cause different problems instead of cure them. Deep, nested menus are equally, if not more, complicated than tree views, because hardly anyone is precise enough with a mouse to keep it in line well enough to move through three or four submenus without error.

So how do we get rid of tree views? And in addressing the need for the deep, nested menu options, how do we Know the Best Ways to Implement It?

The first thing to realize is that we can ditch the root level of the tree entirely. It's not necessary at all.

Here's the tree view interface without the root node, which doesn't help users in any way.

In the tree view, all it tells us is there's some sort of root container that contains everything else. This is pointless when you look at it as a way to choose simple options. If we get rid of the root level, we are left with a list of options. We can display this in a simple list box.

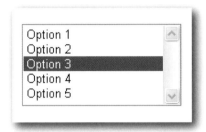

This list box replaces the first layer in the tree view.

The second thing to understand is that the final solution still must offer a way to go on endlessly. You must be able to provide an infinite number of nested options. So we need a solution that just shows an initial set of options, and upon clicking one of them, shows us more options, and on and on until we've located the object we need.

To do this, we can line up several list-boxes in a horizontal row.

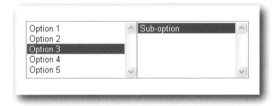

This cascading list-view, with a more obvious menu-style design interface, replaces the tree view.

In case you don't recognize it, this new control is a **cascading list**. Apple uses this paradigm in Mac OS X operating systems, in the Finder application used to navigate the file system on a Mac. It's simply a set of list-box components lined up side by side and bound together with code to display the progression of levels within a hierarchy in a much friendlier way than a tree can offer. Instead of seeing the branches and leaf nodes of a tree, you see *options*. Instead of asking users to learn about the deep, hierarchical nature of the file system, we show *options*. Clicking an option in one column displays another set of options in the next column. Simple as that. There's exactly one way to make a selection using a cascading list. You just click on a label. When you run out of columns, the set of list-boxes scrolls (animates) to the left to hide the first column and simultaneously reveal a fourth.

Amazingly, this style of component has not yet made its way to the Web except in a few rare cases. So here's your call to action: kill the trees. Use cascading lists.

▶ Eliminate Implementation Models

The rest of this chapter is about how to find implementation-model designs in your application plans and eliminate them before they get built. Most of these solutions, such as creating wireframes and running usability tests, are also great as general design methods, but we'll focus on them here as a way to ensure our applications support users' mental models.

Create wireframes to nail things down

When an architect goes to work on a new building, the first major design step is a blueprint. Likewise, when a Web application designer begins a new application, wireframes are often the best place to start. A wireframe is the interface equivalent of a blueprint.

Wireframes come in many shapes and sizes, but they all aim to illustrate the initial design ideas for an end product.

Generally, they're not much more than stick-figure versions of future interface designs. They illustrate layout and spatial relationships, allude to the content that will eventually be added to the interface, and in some cases, show how contrast is to be used to set certain interface elements apart from others.

Various tools can be used to create wireframes, the most popular of which are Microsoft Visio, Adobe Illustrator, and Axure, which I'll talk more about later in this chapter. Each of these tools has its own benefits and shortcomings, but each is a viable option nonetheless.

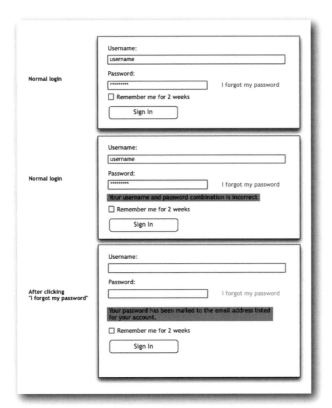

A wireframe of a simple log-in screen has in-line validation to
catch user-name and password errors.

The principle benefit of wireframes is that they help us *design understanding.*
An entire interface can be designed in just a few minutes and changed just
as easily. And you can very quickly end up with a document that shows you
exactly which design elements will impede a user's ability to understand the
application's purpose. You can start with no idea at all about how the interface should look, simply tossing various UI elements onto the screen because
you know they'll need to be there, then gradually refine the layout, organization, and interaction of each element until you have a design that makes sense.
And you can keep going over it until you think the interaction works for users
instead of working only to satisfy the system. (You can ask yourself, for example: Does the user actually need to know when this background operation fails,
or is there a way the application can stay on track without warning the user?
Does this screen need to appear here or somewhere else? Can we get rid of it
entirely? Would getting rid of it make the application easier to understand?)

The Three Rs

When creating wireframes, pay close attention to the following three focal points, which I call the Three Rs.

Requirements. It may seem obvious that you need to pay attention to the requirements of the project, but this R is here as a constant reminder, because it's very easy to let someone else's pet feature (or even your own) make its way into your work. Far better to stick to what's absolutely necessary for the project, to support the activity that the product is meant to support and meet users' goals.

Do not—I repeat—do *not* let things that end with "that would be nice to have" get into your product in the first round. As discussed in Chapter 3, put the nice-to-haves on a separate list and see what's still important later on. For now, when you're staring at your screen and drawing out all the little boxes and widgets that make up your interface, stick to your guns. Stick to what's required. The items that are required are the most important, and are the only ones that should get any attention. The less there is to know about an application, the easier it is to understand.

Reduction. This is my favorite R. Along with sticking to the requirements for the project, be sure to reduce interfaces to their core as much as possible. Reduce clutter, reduce redundancy, reduce the possibility of user error, reduce verbiage until it's only as long as it absolutely needs to be—reduce, reduce, reduce. Then reduce some more. If you can find a way to make a single interface element serve three purposes while maintaining an obvious usage model, do it. If you can turn seven words into two, do it. If you can get rid of an entire interaction because the information it's intended to acquire can be obtained another way, do it, do it, do it.

All of this reduction will result in a significantly more clear and understandable interface. Remember Einstein's rule:

> *Everything should be made as simple as possible,*
> *but not simpler.*

We'll talk about reduction in greater detail in Chapter 8.

Regularity. Regularity is really about making it look like you did things intentionally. It's about using the same font and font size for all form labels, lining up input fields so they create a consistent design, using the same spacing in all blocks of text, the same colors for similar or related interface elements, and so on. Regularity means that if one text field is 20 pixels in from the left edge, and the next one is part of the same form, it should sit 20 pixels in from the left edge as well. Regularity is the notion of organizing, aligning, synchronizing, and optimizing interface elements so that they provide a clear, clean, aesthetically pleasing interface.

Chapter 7 has more on the subject of uniformity, and discusses how to leverage irregularity to create meaning and importance in a design.

The Three Rs are your support system. They keep you in check when your mind starts wandering and you start imagining how cool it would be to add a talking paper clip to your interface that answers help questions. Microsoft has already done this. It wasn't cool. Stick to the Three Rs.

The ultimate goal is to identify places the application can avoid reflecting how the system works. Find ways to avoid asking users questions that satisfy the system's needs instead of theirs. Present the options most likely to be chosen instead of forcing users to choose them manually—default options help illuminate the application's purpose and support the user's purpose. Provide a good starting point instead of forcing users through complicated setup screens, which often ask users tough questions without letting them know they can change their minds later on. Let the application explain itself instead of making the user explain how the system should work.

Wireframes can bring to light a lot of issues you simply can't see otherwise. So create your wireframes, look for the implementation models, and replace them with things that make sense for users.

Kaizen, applied to wireframes

Before you even start creating wireframes, you can grab the nearest notepad and sketch out your ideas there. Firewheel Design did this with Blinksale, and when I asked about the approach, Josh Williams said:

> *We designed 75 percent of the product with ink on paper before we began working on the HTML code itself. This was incredibly helpful as our reasoning was that if the service*

*couldn't be drawn simply on paper it was too complex
for most people to use. The ink sketches also served as a
wonderful reminder of what we wanted the service to be
when we were tempted to add more features later. Of course,
since we launched the service we have added features here
and there, but our goal has always been to keep Blinksale
easy to use for everybody.*

The first step I usually take is to sketch several design possibilities on a white-board (a dry-erase board). I sometimes do this in collaboration with other people involved with a particular project, but often it's just me and a marker. I simply swing my chair around from my desk and start frantically draw-ing something out on the large whiteboard conveniently (and intentionally) located on the wall two feet behind me.

Some people stop there. If you're designing and building the application your-self, you can certainly go straight from a sketch to the real thing, even if you're only coding the HTML end of things.

The problem with this is that few people, if any, can consistently design the best possible interaction on the first try by simply sketching it out on a piece of paper once and going straight to code. The people who can do this under-stand complicated systems and have a far deeper knowledge of computer interactions than the average computer user.

Use cases and wireframes help designers see problems with an interface early on in the process and help them think through it. Designers are forced to think about each and every screen, how they relate to each other, how they flow, and how users might grasp them.

As a result, creativity is given a bigger seat at the table.

Ideas emerge when designers give themselves the space they need to come up with them. If you only give yourself one shot to sketch something out before you start coding, you'll rarely see the other possibilities. But if your goal is to lay out an entire application and hand it off to a team of developers, then the entire process may begin and end with wireframes.

For example, I sketch ideas on the whiteboard, then move to Axure or PowerPoint, or whatever tool might be best that day, and create a fairly detailed wireframe there. Then I go into **kaizen** mode.

Kaizen, again, translates to "improvement." In Web terms, it's the equivalent of practicing iterative design (discussed in Chapters 2 and 8).

Before I hand the wireframes off for review and approval, I go over them several times, just as I do with use cases, each time trying to find ways to improve task flows, make UI widgets more clear, and error-proof the screens (we'll talk about this more in Chapter 6).

Recently, while revamping the editing features in a Web page-builder application to improve usability, I immediately saw many ways that menus and toolbar options could be consolidated to clean up the interface. So I created a text document and started making notes about all the things that could be grouped together, options that could be removed from the main toolbar, and pop-up windows that could be eliminated. I also took out my sketchpad and sketched out what the interface would look like if all these things were done.

Yes, it was much simpler than before, but it just wasn't enough. There were still two different modes for editing a newly created Web page, and neither of them kept users in context—they both either took users away from the main interface or changed the view of the interface substantially enough that it was difficult to understand how edits would affect the page when they were completed. So I started looking for ways to combine the two editing modes and keep them in the main interface so that users would only have to learn that *what you see is what you get.* Plus, if a user could edit the page directly instead of moving into another mode, she would be able to work with the tool with a much simpler mental model.

In doing this, I saw a way to create a main toolbar that offered up a few common features and a couple of menus, and show it every time a user clicked into an editable text block. But after creating a first draft of a wireframe, this still seemed a bit awkward, as it meant this toolbar would appear in a different place every time the user edited a different area of a page.

Because users tend to rely on spatial memory—that is, they memorize where something is located on a page and continue to go back to the same spot for the functionality they found there last time—moving the toolbar around all the time wouldn't be an effective solution. After a little toying around with the wireframe, I moved the toolbar into a permanent spot within the main interface, and then added tabs to it. Each tab contained the editing tools for different page elements. One contained text-formatting tools. Another contained form widgets so users could add a form to their page and edit the properties of each form element. Another tab contained image-editing tools. Each tab provided a way to add elements to a Web page a user would create himself, and the toolbar as a whole was contextual, so that when the user clicked inside a text block, he would see the text-formatting tab, and when he selected an image, he would see the image-editing tab, and so on.

This solution was by far the best of the possibilities, as it eliminated several implementation-model designs (such as the pop-up window used for one of the editing modes, which took users *away* from the page being edited), provided the right tools at the right time, and allowed me to get rid of many points of duplicate functionality. By doing these things, the new design made the tool easier to understand.

I never would have seen this possibility if I had drawn up one sketch and gone straight to code. The moral of the story is that even if you do decide to go straight from sketch to code, don't rely on the first sketch. Go through a few and give yourself room to see the possibilities in a design before committing to anything.

Once I'm comfortable with a design, I hand it off to another interface designer to get a second opinion. When that's done, it goes to that application's product manager so we can hash out any other issues. (Eventually, the wireframes are approved, sent to graphic designers to be turned into final artwork, and then handed to developers to be built.)

All in all, the wireframes are probably changed ten times before they go to the development team. (Doing the same thing with code could take hours. In more extreme cases, two hours spent on wireframe revisions can eliminate weeks of coding. Unlike code, wireframes are extremely simple and inexpensive to change.) Each iteration is an incremental improvement over the previous version, and each one is a step closer to an obvious design that reflects a user's model instead of one that reflects only what the underlying system needs to perform its routines.

▶ Prototype the Design

A prototype is essentially the interactive version of a set of wireframes, by which other people can see how an interaction might work, how they might navigate a site to get through a series of screens, or how a particular widget, such as a drag-and-drop shopping cart, might behave. Prototypes come in varying degrees of quality, and it doesn't really matter how you build your prototypes, how nice they are, or whether they're exact simulations of a future design. What matters is that they demonstrate how something should work to some reasonable degree of accuracy.

The prime benefit of a prototype is that it brings to the surface all the instances where the system's logic is dictating how a design comes together (plus it gives you something to show clients and coworkers that actually functions). Clients, and you, can click on interface elements, see what happens as a result, and begin to get a real sense of what an application or site will do. This makes it quite simple to spot implementation models in a design, because they're right in front of you and there's no way to escape them. And seeing them is the first step toward getting rid of them.

In addition to giving clients something that they can touch and use, a prototype can be used to solicit feedback about an interface before you get too deep into the process to make adjustments. Writing code is expensive, and it takes valuable time and energy to make changes to a working application. Making substantial changes late in the game causes missed deadlines and overblown budgets, but changing the entire behavior of an interaction in a prototype is fast, cheap, and easy. And usually it only takes one person to build and maintain the prototype, so it doesn't even interrupt a project.

The simple fact is that a prototype allows you to get valuable feedback and put it into action immediately to see how the new version is received. If people don't like the next version of the prototype, you can easily change it again. In fact, you can change it several times in a matter of hours, exploring different solutions to each problem the prototype is meant to address, and nail down a final solution before getting into coding.

Another key advantage to prototyping is that you have an interface in front of you throughout the entire development process, which helps limit the addition of new features that might obscure the basic purpose of the tool and therefore impinge on the user's mental model. It also provides a clear picture of how the final project will work so everyone knows exactly what needs to be done, and it gives you a chance to work with the product directly very early in the process so you can gradually refine, step by step by step, until it shines.

Note, however, that it's best to avoid using prototype code in a finished application. Prototype code is generally hacked together in a very short period of time and usually doesn't provide the scalability needed to create a stable application.

One last benefit of a prototype is that you can create usability tests around it early in the development process. As long as your prototype clearly shows what will happen at each step in a process, you can run it past some actual users and find out very quickly what problems exist, what questions come up, and what can be improved. We'll talk more about testing your application later in this chapter.

There are quite a few ways to create a prototype, and each style has its own pros and cons. Following is a breakdown of some popular prototyping styles.

Paper prototyping

A paper prototype is made up of interface elements sketched on different pieces of paper so that various application states and screens can be shown without redrawing the interface each time. A paper prototype can be used for early usability tests by having one person act as the computer and another as the test moderator. The user "clicks" (touches) the parts of the interface he wants to interact with and the person acting as the computer manipulates the paper sketches to show what would happen in the application as a result. To learn more about paper prototyping, pick up Carolyn Snyder's book *Paper Prototyping: The Fast and Easy Way to Design and Refine User Interfaces* (2003), and read every last word.

HTML

HTML prototypes are Web pages put together without regard for color, fonts, or anything else that qualifies as a detail. The goal is to simply get the major elements of a screen into a basic HTML format and have users test it out to see if they understand the application's basic purpose and flow and interaction model. Various WYSIWYG (what-you-see-is-what-you-get) editors like Adobe Dreamweaver can be used to create these incredibly stripped-down versions of application screens in very little time, and it's a great way to see how an application might really work once it's completed so you can rapidly shape it into something that supports a user's mental model.

Click-through mockups

A click-through mockup is a series of mockups that illustrate various application states or screens, each of which has triggers (such as a button) to transport the user to the next screen and illustrate a basic task flow. Prototypes like this are great for illustrating a single course of action, but aren't always very efficient for simulating multiple interactions within a single interface, or multiple states within a single screen. In other words, it might be nice to use a click-through mockup to show the progression from one step in a paginated form to the next, but you probably wouldn't want to use it to demonstrate a page with multiple possible actions, each of which leads to different screens. Stick to showing off a single interaction rather than trying to create something as dynamic as what you might be able to show with a more robust prototype. Still, click-through mockups can help you see where implementation models are being used so you can change things now instead of later.

Flash

Flash is a fantastic tool for prototyping, but only if you know your way around ActionScript and can whip up interfaces quickly using the UI Component Set that ships with the authoring tool and any prototype elements that need to be built from scratch. If you're willing to dive in, or already have some Flash skill, it's definitely worth testing to see if it's right for you. Create a prototype for something simple, such as a contact form, and see how far you have to take things to create an effective sample. The benefits you gain from the rich interface capabilities of Flash can outweigh the extra time you'll need to create prototypes with it.

▶ Test It Out

The number one way to explore the user experience of an application once it's created—and find any remaining implementation-model designs—is to test it. You've heard the hype about usability testing, you've read an article or two, and you may have even tried it, but odds are you're not testing your applications as often or in as many ways as you should be because, you might think, usability testing is typically very expensive and time-consuming. But there are plenty of ways to perform tests and get the information you need to build a better application, and the benefits reach far and wide. Abe Fettig, the man behind JotSpot, says:

> *Having users involved throughout the process was very helpful because it helped us identify any problems with the product. If we were missing an important feature, or something in the UI was confusing, or there was an irritating bug, we'd hear about it, usually from more than one person. Bringing in new testers throughout the development process was especially valuable because it gave us the perspective of people using the product for the first time. That helped us to recognize parts of the UI that were confusing to new users.*

The browserless self-test

A surefire way to get some quick feedback on your site is to test it yourself using the **browserless self-test**. *Browserless* is my word for testing without the benefit of browser tools. All you need to do is hide the tools in your browser, so you can't rely on <u>Back</u> and <u>Forward</u> buttons, an address bar, a refresh or reload button, or bookmarks.

Each browser comes with a way to hide all its tools. The option to hide each of these tools is usually tucked away in the View menu. Simply select the appropriate menu option to disable each of the various toolbars and you're ready to go.

Once you've gone browserless, you can find out how good your navigation really is—you can gauge how well it tells users where things are and how to get things done. (If your design is filled with implementation-model information architecture, this will be more difficult, as a system's logical groupings and associations are usually very different than a user's).

Lay out a series of tasks to perform, such as "Purchase a rubber duckie" and "Find a desk lamp." Then run through each task to see if you can get around easily. You'll quickly find that going browserless is a little like cutting off your right hand. You never realize how much you rely on the back and forward buttons until you lose them. Suddenly, you realize that in order to go back, you have to remember the name of the page you were on, be able to use a link to get it, and be confident that the link you click is the right one. Of course, you can cheat a little by using the backspace or delete key to go back, but try to keep yourself from doing this. Most people don't even know about this shortcut, and cheating won't help you make your site better.

Finding a page within the site is easier to do if it has a clear, relevant title that maps directly to a link on the page you're viewing now. If the link can't use the exact page title of the page it links to, it needs to instill at least enough confidence that users can tell they'll go right to it by clicking the link. If the page cannot be linked to directly from every other page, then users need to be able to *eventually* get to the page they're after by following a path through the site.

Browserless self-tests help support a user's mental model by forcing you to see how the site is really organized. If your site holds up against this test, odds are the organizational structure is pretty solid.

For example, an About the Company page will probably be linked to in the persistent navigation on your site. Almost every page will contain this link and users can always find it. But a product information page about the rubber duckie you want to buy, on a site that sells thousands of different products, isn't going to be so prevalent. To find the duckie, you need to be able to wade through the architecture of the entire site. You might start by doing a simple search using the site's search function. If the search results are good, you'll find the duckie in no time. If the results aren't good, because the underlying database isn't designed with the same conceptual groups and this design flaw made its way to the site's navigation, or if there is no Search box, or you're not sure what keywords to use in your search, you might click the **Products** link, choose the **Rubber Toys** category link on the landing page, and then choose a particular rubber duckie from the category's main catalog page.

What this means is that every page needs to not only provide access to the products catalog, but also be incredibly clear that the link leads to information about your products not information about the fact that you sell products, how you sell them, or how you ship them, but a page that starts the process of drilling down into the site hierarchy to find the rubber duckie.

Here's Target.com without the aid of browser tools like back and forward buttons.

Using Target.com in a browserless test to locate a desk lamp, I landed on a page full of desk lamps in exactly *two clicks* by choosing **Home Office** from the Furniture drop-down menu in the persistent navigation, and then clicking **Desk Lamps** in the sidebar navigation on the landing page. Nice.

This could have been a lucky guess, however, so I tried another method. I chose **Lighting** from the Home drop-down menu in the persistent navigation and then clicked **See All** under the **Desk Lamps** category in the sidebar navigation. I ended up on the very same page. Still two clicks. *Very nice.*

Well done, Target.com. Someone there is focused on my mental model.

The five-second test

User Interface Engineering (**www.uie.com**) advocates the use of what they call the "five-second test." This type of usability testing involves gathering up some users, or going somewhere many people are likely to be gathered at once (they suggest the company's cafeteria). So it's slightly more complicated than a browserless self-test, but the focus is very different, as it is intended to yield insights about the clarity of a site.

To perform a five-second test, write a list of screens on your site or in your application that need to be particularly clear and concise, and either open them up in different browser windows (or tabs within a single window) or print them out and show them to the users. Show each user the screens, one at a time, for five seconds each, and ask them to write down notes about everything they saw.

A prime candidate for a five-second test is a page that has only one purpose and is critical to the success of the site. For example, a page on a domain-name registrar's site that lets users search for domain names—the key product for the company—should be crystal clear, because making the domain-search function and purchase path difficult to understand would seriously affect the company's sales. Ask each user to look at the screen for five seconds. When the five seconds are up, have the users write down everything they remember about the page. Ask them what they think is the focus of the page. Ask them what the domain extension options were. Ask them what they'd click to choose a domain extension.

If you get the answers you want, you're doing well. If not, it's a sign you should redesign the page. Don't perform a major redesign on it, though, unless it's really off the mark—just apply incremental changes to it until it works. The goal is usually to incrementally reduce clutter in this design until the point of the screen becomes clear. We'll talk more about reducing clutter in Chapter 8.

For more information on five-second tests, see UIE's article at **www.uie. com/articles/five_second_test**.

Interview testing

A more complicated, but more in-depth approach to usability testing is to perform interview-style sessions. These are done by meeting with users in person, asking them to complete various tasks in an application, and have them think out loud about what they experience so you can determine how the application holds up to the user's mental model. Typically, interview sessions require three to eight users and last several days, but they can be reduced to two or three users with all the tests performed in a single morning.

These types of sessions involve more planning than other tests. Prior to performing a usability session like this, you need to plan a set of tasks that users will be asked to complete, prepare a lab of some kind—a room where you can perform the tests and record the sessions (preferably on video, using a video camera or a screen-recording tool like Camtasia or TechSmith's product, Morae)—and schedule users to come to your company.

Preparing tasks to be tested can be time-consuming, because the ideal tasks are those that satisfy the key business objectives while also fitting in with a user's goals. For example, a stock photography site might have a key business objective to establish a large base of repeat visitors, while the user's goal might be to find a quicker way to get through a site's thousands of images. To meet these goals, the application might enable a user to add any image she sees to a personal library so that on future visits she can go straight to a small set of images she already knows she likes. The tasks of creating and using the personal library are perfect for usability testing. If a user doesn't understand the core concept of the personal library or how to work with it, the goals of the application cannot be met. Through active listening and the use of surveys taken by users before and after the session about how they felt about the application while using it, you can extract quite a bit of insight about how understandable the application is, and you're likely to learn a few things you weren't even thinking about.

Recruiting testers

One thing to note here is that finding users to test is sometimes tricky. Some companies use marketing agencies to handle this, because they keep detailed profile information on hand and can simply pull up a list of people who fit the profile for the test session. Then the agencies handle calling all those people and scheduling as many as the company needs. This has a cost, of course, but it can be a big time-saver. If you have a product support department within your company, however, you can try to leverage that fact by getting the support people to help you sign up and schedule testers. You might also add a link to your site that lets people know they can get involved in improving future versions of your product by volunteering for usability tests. This link should direct users to a screening survey on your site to help determine ahead of time who might be good for a particular testing session. You can leave this up all the time, in fact, provided you have a way to manage the pool of users that will be generated by it. Doing this, you can simply pull up a list anytime you want to run a new test, make a few calls, and you've got yourself a testing session.

(By the way, don't forget to compensate the users somehow. Gift cards, free software, things like that. Give users a reason to get involved.)

Contextual usability testing

Interview-style testing can have one major downside, in that users tend to open their critical eye while participating in usability testing sessions, which can obscure the truth about the test results. Despite telling them you're testing the software and not them, users tend to think they need to be thorough and mention every little thing they come across, and this isn't really how people work with applications in their own environments. Also, the fact that the testers are in lab settings means they won't know certain information about the computer they're using, such as bandwidth settings and what (fake) credit card number to use if they'll be making a purchase as part of the test. This can throw off the tester and interrupt the testing session.

To avoid all this, and potentially gain more honest feedback, you can try **contextual usability testing**, (a.k.a. *reconnaissance testing*). This involves watching users interact with your product without telling them that you're taking mental notes about how they're using it. You can do this by asking people within your company to walk you through a certain task under the ruse that you don't already know how to complete it, or simply walk over and strike up a conversation with someone using the product and ask what they're up to.

Of course, you run the risk they'll stop working while you're talking to them, and that won't be any good at all. To prevent this, you could just eavesdrop from behind a nearby rubber tree plant. Pretend you're reading something and just listen to the user complain to her neighbor about how difficult it is to find a rubber duckie on your site. Or bring the test to the user under the ruse that you need it double-checked for typos, broken links, and so on (a.k.a. *bulletproofing*). Watch for what confuses users and what irritates them. Do they gradually get more frustrated, for example, when asked the same question ("Are you sure?") every time they delete data within the application? If so, the implementation model is winning again, and you know what needs to be done.

Keep the "tests" informal and in context. Perform usability tests the same way you perform contextual inquiry. Then ask the users what they thought of the overall experience, and employ active listening to bear out the critical information they are dying to give you.

Eat your own dog food

Eating your own dog food is the act of using the products you create, as religiously as your customers. It's a very simple idea.

It is also the single most effective method I've found yet not only to test an application, but also to get an up-close and personal look at the experience I'm forcing upon my users. It pays off in ways that cannot easily be described. You simply have to do it to understand just how great it is.

Consider this story.

My local library recently changed its domain name. No big deal. But to avoid the incredible marketing and customer education campaign that would be needed to inform patrons of the change, they opted to redirect users to the new site automatically. Instead of redirecting users from every page of the old site, however, only the library's home page was pointed to the new location. If every user went straight to the home page, and all the bookmarks that patrons had ever created went only to the home page, this would have worked. But this wasn't so.

On the day after the switch, librarians all over the district were inundated with phone calls—far more than normal—from customers saying said they couldn't log in. Others said they couldn't even access the log-in page.

All of these customers had bookmarked the log-in page. The rather obvious fact, which no one involved with the creation and maintenance of the site realized, is that the vast majority of library patrons go to the site to perform tasks involved with their accounts. The home page offered no way to log in, so it wasn't the page they used. The log-in page, on the other hand, wasn't redirecting them to the new domain.

The logical thing to do when a site provides account access is to provide a log-in widget on the home page. That's the obvious design. The library did not do this. Its understanding of how users worked with the site didn't match how users actually worked. The solution was based on the system. The system says the home page is the major entry point to the site, so it's the page that was redirected. In other words, the library had a dysfunctional mental model of its users.

If the library's Web team had been eating their own dog food, they would have known about the issue long before that fateful day when all those customers were suddenly stuck with no ability to log in to their accounts. They could have avoided the issue completely and improved the user experience for *all* of their customers in the meantime.

When you use an application yourself, it's very hard to trap yourself into theoretical, academic conversations about whether Solution A is more usable than Solution B. You get to see the problems firsthand. In addition to giving you an inside perspective on what it's like to be a user of your application, it's also incredibly motivating, because you're in a position to fix the issues.

Only by eating your own dog food can you really see what's great, what needs work, what needs to be added, and what needs to be removed. Sure, you can learn some of these things by simply doing quality assurance testing prior to release, but QA is not personal. When you use an application every single day, it becomes very personal. It's part of your life. You use it to complete the very same tasks your users do. And since it's your application, you can actually make it better.

All in all, there are a million ways to uncover how users think about an application and implement solutions that meet those needs. Sketches, wireframes, prototypes, and usability tests are all great ways to find those pesky implementation-model designs and replace them with something more in line with a user's mental model. Focusing on these things will make your applications better. And better applications make for happier users who keep coming back.

5

Turn Beginners Into Intermediates, Immediately

▶ Use Up-to-Speed Aids

▶ Choose Good Defaults

▶ Design for Information

▶ Stop Getting Up to Speed and Speed Things Up

▶ Provide Help Documents, Because Help Is for Experts

When we, the more computer-savvy users of the world, dive into a new application, we tend to learn everything we can as quickly as possible, hunting through all the nooks and crannies to uncover features and find out how the application stands up to others we've used. We want to see how far we can push the application. We strive to become experts.

Other people don't do this. They get up to speed just enough to become productive with the application, and they stay at this level until there's a compelling reason to learn more. Usually, there is no compelling reason.

Alan Cooper points out in *The Inmates Are Running the Asylum* that the skill level of users doesn't break down quite as neatly as we usually think, into beginner, intermediate, and expert. First of all, most users are not experts. In fact, only a very small percentage of users ever extend their skills within an application beyond that of an intermediate user. Secondly, beginners tend to quickly learn what they need to know to use an application, stepping forward at great speed into the land of what Cooper calls "perpetual intermediates."

What this means is that when we design for beginners and/or experts, we're usually designing for the wrong crowd. The intermediate users are by far the largest group.

Even when an intermediate user does become an expert, it's often for a very short period of time, when the application being used is particularly important for a certain project or task where the user has to spend a substantial amount of time using it, and therefore learns to use it with greater proficiency.

Focusing on the features intermediate users want and need means improving usability all around by leaving out many of the more obscure features that take a long time to create and learn. Building less also translates to shorter time lines, so we can get applications to market sooner and spend less money doing it. (Isn't it nice, by the way, how well the concepts of improving usability and getting to market quickly work together? It's ironic, but often the less time you spend building an application, the better it is.)

Along the way, however, we have to remember to teach our future intermediate users how to use our applications, or they'll never become intermediates. We also have to remember that since we're designing for intermediates, continually shoving beginner-level tools in their way will annoy them in the long run.

To satisfy both goals, we need to offer up some sacrificial lambs, so to speak. That is, we need to implement some tools that stick around long enough to help users learn what they need to know, but then disappear once their purpose has been served. We also need to make smart decisions about which features to put up front and which ones to tuck away in the back. We need to inject instructive elements into interfaces that help new users and serve as reminders to intermediate users. Finally, we need to provide help documentation for the users who will eventually read it, and instructive hints throughout the application so everyone can be productive without a lot of hassle.

▶ Use Up-to-Speed Aids

Getting users up to speed in Web applications is something that needs to be handled on a case-by-case basis. There isn't one best way to do it. But there are plenty of ways we can get it done via the use of "up-to-speed" aids.

For example, we can provide a Getting Started guide to new users and display a link to it when a user logs in for the first time. We can offer a video tour that shows new users a quick overview of the product's main feature set. In an application where users collectively contribute to a large base of information, like a wiki, we can point users to examples of content created by other users so they can see the end result of the work they're being asked to perform.

Getting Started guides and video tours, however, are used out of context. Users can't read information about how an application works at the same time they're using the application because the two usually appear in different windows. In an application where examples of content can be shown to new users, the examples generally don't offer insight into how the content was created, so users still need information about how to get going and how to complete basic tasks. And this is a prime moment for us as application developers, because if a user is looking around for a way to get started, it means we've already convinced her that our application is worth trying out. Now is the time to pounce and show the user what we've got.

Many applications resort to walking new users through **wizards**, which are step-by-step sequences of screens designed to get a user to configure the initial settings for an application. The least objectionable of these offer insight into how to use the application along the way. The most objectionable have a few common bad habits.

First, wizards tend to ask questions about how a user wishes to use the application right off the bat. The problem is that the user has never previously used the application, so answering such questions, while not impossible, is purely speculative on the user's part. The next problem is that wizards rarely assure users that they can change their decisions later on. But worse than this is that the presence of a wizard is a clear sign the application designers haven't made good decisions for users in the first place. Users may not catch on to this, but they will catch on to the fact that the wizard is keeping them from *playing around with the application.*

If we manage to convince a user to check out an application, the next logical step is to get them moving forward. Quickly.

Marketing master Seth Godin recognized this challenge when approaching the design of Squidoo (**www.squidoo.com**). He recently told me:

> *Designing Squidoo was difficult. It was difficult because there's a lot to say, a lot to teach, a lot to demonstrate, but just a fraction of a second to do it. When introducing a website to the public, you are not presenting them with a toolbox. You're telling a story. If the story is appealing and coherent—if it leaps off the screen and makes someone want to hear more of it—then you get a chance to show off your tools and features and benefits. But if your story is too dense or scary, they're gone.*

Squidoo is an information-sharing application with which users tie together disparate bits of information to create a **lens** (a Squidoo content page) to make it findable via Squidoo's LensRank search engine.

Someone interested in insects, for example, who has a blog about bugs and has spent some time collecting links to various resources on the topic, could create a lens that links to each resource and displays the page creator's most recent blog posts. Anyone interested in insects could do a search on the subject in Squidoo, find the insect lens, and learn a bunch of information in one place.

Great idea, Seth.

Squidoo does an excellent job of getting users up to speed, constantly providing helpful hints about how to do things, and it even branches off to a second Web site that offers tips and tricks for improving lenses and marketing them. There's also a simple FAQ section that explains most of what you need to know to get going in Squidoo, complete with suggestions about how it can help promote your new book, nonprofit organization, or weekly podcast.

(If this isn't enough to convince you to start using Squidoo, by the way, the FAQ section also explains how to get *paid* for building lenses.)

Squidoo provides a page to title and tag your lens.

When adding modules to a new lens (RSS and Links List sections, for example), you see a screen listing loads of module types organized by what's new, what's most popular, and which ones help you make money. There is also an index of all module types so you can find what you need even if it's not in the main categories. There's also a Search box so you can find a module type without hunting through the index. Choosing module types to add to your new lens builds a list farther down on the page so you can keep track of what you've added. Clicking the **Save** button creates your new lens and presents all the modules you added so you can begin editing them.

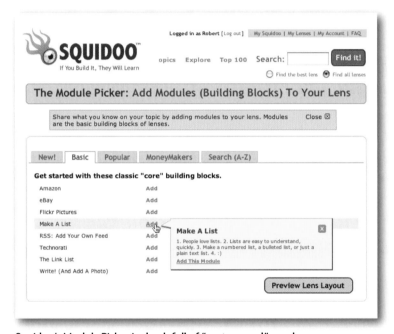

Squidoo's Module Picker is chock full of "up-to-speed" goodness.

Each module features a large Edit button, prompting you to start filling the modules with content. When you click **Edit**, the form used to edit the module magically appears just below the Edit button via the use of Dynamic HTML.

Everything in the Create Custom Lens page guides the user toward the successful creation of a new lens, and everything in the lens-editing screen guides the user toward filling it up with content. There are large, easy-to-spot buttons, on-demand editing features that can be accessed without leaving the page, and bits of instructive text throughout the page to alleviate confusion about anything not completely clear.

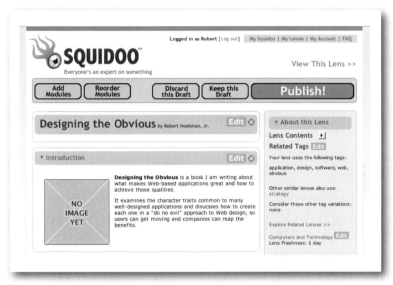

Large, clearly labeled buttons tell users exactly what to do and how.

These and other elements like them help users get up to speed quickly and start building Squidoo lenses.

Provide a welcome screen

Many desktop-installed applications—Adobe Dreamweaver and Flash, for example—provide welcome screens to new users. These screens often offer links to a quick tour of a tool's feature set and tutorials to get started. That's awfully nice of them, but again, these types of aids are used out of context from the application and end up not being as helpful as they could be. Yes, people can learn in one window and apply new knowledge in other windows, but users can only focus on one window at a time. And a window containing a tutorial is not an application window, so users are focusing in the wrong place. It's better to train users by having them actually use the application.

To build a better welcome screen, we need to *Know The Best Ways To Implement It*. Instead of offering tours and tutorials out of context, a welcome screen should be integrated into the application screens themselves and remain contextual. For example, we can designate an area at the top of an application screen to display information about what to do on that page and perhaps what to do next. We can also reveal new information whenever a user switches screens. Keeping it contextual like this means each and every screen in the application can teach users how to perform tasks without preventing them from using it at the same time.

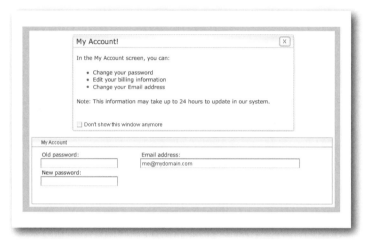

An integrated welcome screen informs users of what they can do on the My Account page.

Welcome screens implemented like this should, of course, offer an obvious way for users to disable the screen so it doesn't appear on repeat visits. A simple check box lets users close the welcome screen easily and be on their way.

Offer tips

We can also offer a method to display tips. These can appear whenever users come across a new feature, just in case other instructive design elements (covered later in this chapter) aren't enough for the user to start being productive. Users who feel more comfortable with Web applications, of course, can choose to turn the tips off and proceed at their own risk, but new users who might benefit from the tips have a simple way to get help whenever they need it the first few times they use the application.

Fly-out tip balloons like this one from Box.net offer users assistance right when they need it.

Box (www.box.net), an online file-storage application, offers both a welcome screen and an inline tips feature. With tips enabled, rolling over particular areas of the application screen displays callouts containing explanations of what feature is offered in that area and how to use it.

Tips should be kept short and to the point. The object is to help users, not interfere with their workflow by asking them to read long blocks of text that keep them from moving forward. Concise and vigorous writing is definitely the way to go.

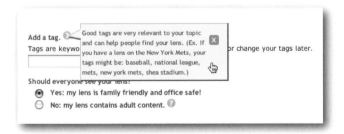

Users gain access to Squidoo's inline help via question mark icons.

Squidoo is also quite good at providing inline help. Question mark icons appear next to each element on the Create Lens screen that requires further explanation. For example, an inline tip is offered to help new users understand the purpose of tags in Squidoo and how to leverage them. Tips presented like this stay out of everyone's way while still providing quick access to useful information for users who want to learn to improve their pages.

Fill the blank slate with something useful

A blank slate can be a scary thing. It's a big empty space where there will eventually be content you create yourself. It's a blank sheet of sketch paper. In a Web application, it's often a page with no content that the user is supposed to fill.

Some people are inspired by spaces like these. I'm one of them. When I look at a blank slate, I "see" all the things I want to put in it. Many designers can do this. But for users just getting to know a Web application, a blank slate can be a barrier in the learning process. Instead of knowing exactly what to do first, users can become stalled when faced with the empty canvas.

To eliminate these moments of "stuckness," it's good to fill the blank slate with something useful. In addition to helping users get up to speed, it can be a great way to compel users to jump in and start using the application, which can be the hardest thing to do. The first few moments users spend with a new application can be intimidating. Again, the goal is to get them moving forward quickly.

When asked how 37signals gets users going in new applications, Jason Fried told me:

> *Have them dive in. Experiment. Use them. Make mistakes, even. Don't throw a big manual on someone's desk and say "READ THIS!"—that will only set them up for an ugly experience. Software shouldn't be something you have to use, it should be something you want to use. When you have to train people to use something, or when you force them to read page after page, software becomes a chore. Not good. So make simple software that doesn't require a manual and let people derive immediate value from your product by encouraging them to just dive in.*

37signals makes the act of jumping in very simple. In applications like Basecamp and Backpack, it's easy to know exactly what to do as soon as you log in for the first time, because there is no blank slate. Instead, there is a very noticeable block of text or an image that explains what to do, like a help document that appears exactly when and where you need it.

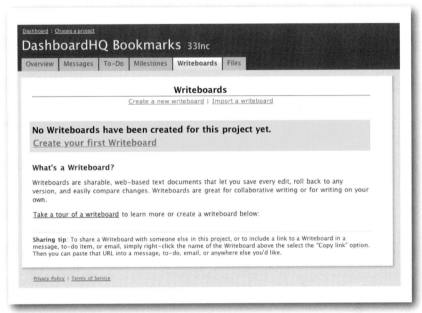

Basecamp's blank slate features a giant red text link that guides users toward adding content.

Yahoo! offers something similar the first time a user visits My Yahoo (my.yahoo.com), one of the many start-page applications on the Web designed to give users an at-a-glance view of news, weather, RSS feeds, and other things. Some default content has been added to the page, but since the new My Yahoo user hasn't yet selected the content he wants to see, the sample page is disabled and a large preview graphic is positioned in the upper-left corner of the washed-out sample content so he knows exactly what his page will eventually contain.

My Yahoo shows users what their page could look like after just a few minutes
of playing around with the application.

First impressions are vital, especially on the Web, where the competition is
just a click away and we have only a few seconds to convince users that our
applications are worth using. Showing users ahead of time exactly what they
get when they invest a few minutes in our applications can make them comfortable, eager to dive in, and immediately knowledgeable.

These are all good things. Not only do users get to feel productive and smart,
we get to keep another customer.

Give instructive hints

Another effective way to help users get moving, now *and* later, is to apply a
little **instructive design**. Instructive text, for example, can be used in form elements and interfaces in general to guide the user within the context of her
current task without being intrusive.

A text field that accepts only a numerical value can display a sample value of 0. The sample value is displayed so users can clearly see what type of information is required and enter the right type of data without having to think about it or guess. This small bit of instructive design helps guide users toward completing a task or through the use of an interaction without interfering with workflow. It simply eliminates questions in the user's mind before they come up.

Instructive text can also be used as an inline tip about how to perform a certain action or what happens as a result of performing an action.

When providing tips in an interface (for example, a line of instruction about what will happen when the user interacts with the page element), instructive text should be set to a small font size—smaller than the default font size for the text in the rest of the page—and simply positioned near enough to the interaction to which it applies that the connection is obvious. The goal, ultimately, is to get rid of the little thought bubbles that appear over users' heads that say things like, "Um, what's this button do?"

Instructive text can be used in these cases:

1. When a form field requires a specific data type (such as a number) and it is potentially unclear to users what needs to be entered.

2. When users are expected to enter a value in a specific format (such as "123456-A").

3. When it is unclear what the result of an action will be or how to perform an action (for example, "Click inside the text block to specify where the new text should be inserted").

When a default value is offered within a form field, the dummy text should be shown in a midtone gray font instead of the default black so the user knows the text is only there as a guide. But when this text is instructive (that is, it tells the user what to do instead of showing a default value), it's not usually necessary to change the font color. And when the field gains focus—when a user clicks or tabs into the field—the instructive text should disappear immediately so the user can begin typing.

Dashboard HQ, a simple bookmark manager (produced by my partnership, 33Inc), uses instructional text inside form elements to let users know what new content needs to be entered.

Kiko, an application for managing a personal calendar, does a good job of using instructive text to help users understand some of the less obvious components in the tool.

Kiko includes a legend in its sidebar that explains exactly what each element means.

To explain what clicking on various appointment labels does, for example, Kiko uses inline tips. Ironically, these tips appear as thought bubbles. In this case, however, the thought bubbles are on the page instead of in the user's head.

JotSpot Live does a good job here as well. JotSpot Live is a collaborative note-taking tool designed to allow groups of users to contribute notes from meetings and such to one common Web page that can be accessed later on and used to maintain an archive of the notes.

The "Click here to add text" statement positioned in the center of new text blocks on a JotSpot Live page serves to tell new users exactly what needs to be done to add a new note, and gives experienced users a visual clue to where the next text block begins. This text block also uses a different background color than others in the page to make it stand out even more. A quick glance at the page reveals exactly where to add the next note.

JotSpot Live also offers icons that are quite helpful on their own, and these are another good example of instructive design elements. Clicking into a text block to create a new note presents several text-formatting options, each of which is represented by an icon that explains what it does. Leveraging a user's experience with text-editing tools like Microsoft Word, the application offers icon-style buttons to apply various styles to the text, such as bold, italic, underline, and strikethrough, as well as hyperlinks.

A quick click of the **Save** link saves the new note, restores the page to its original state, and produces a new editable text block.

Instructive hints come in many forms, but all of them show up just in time and keep users on track, alleviating confusion and frustration.

Interface Surgery: Applying instructive design

Users expect feedback when they interact with computers. In fact, they generally expect the same level of feedback from computers as they would get from real people in real situations. If a user is supposed to answer a set of questions, for example, she'll expect some feedback that the system can use the answers as she provided them and that she's moving forward in the process.

Forms don't usually supply this feedback. Instead, users often complete a form in its entirety without getting any feedback at all until the end, when users are told they've entered data in a way the system can't handle. When it comes to forms, typically users only get feedback if they mess something up.

This happens often when users enter email addresses and phone numbers, among other things. A user can get all the way through a page-long form and click the Submit button feeling pretty confident she's going to see a positive result. Instead, she sees a JavaScript alert message telling her the phone number she entered is in an incorrect format, or the page refreshes and displays a list of the errors that must be addressed before she can move on.

This is not a good way to reinforce positive behavior on the user's part. And it can be rather insulting to have a computer tell you that you're not conforming to its rules. Isn't the computer a tool that helps you instead of the other way around?

Lots of companies have heeded the call to make their applications more usable and have leapt into action, but sadly, many of them are just redesigning bad behavior. One of my favorite examples is the registration form on Odeo.com, a podcast aggregation and creation service.

Odeo's registration form is definitely simple. It doesn't ask for any information it doesn't actually need. It asks for only three pieces of information: name, email address, and password (though they ask you to confirm the password you're setting, so you have to enter it twice). But the problem isn't with the simplicity, it's with the size.

The image shown here may not do it justice. The important thing to notice is that the four form fields are *huge*. Maybe Odeo's designers thought they were improving the usability of the form by making it readable from across the room. Maybe they just wanted to fill up the space. Who knows. Whatever the case, they didn't do any of the things we can do as application designers and developers to make the form truly more effective, so their apparent intention to improve usability ends up looking like an insult. It's as though they're saying to all the less computer-savvy users out there, which they appear to be rather tired of, "Go ahead. Just try to screw *this* up!"

Most users won't have problems seeing the form. Making it big won't help. Let's take a look at what *will* help.

First take a look at this rather typical form used to store contact information.

One generic form, served up fresh.

Nothing special here. Looks like 1,000 other forms we've all seen (and probably created).

The form is one of the most common interactions on the Web, used for everything from purchasing airlines tickets to signing up for an Amazon account. And while they're usually simple enough to get through, they tend to exhibit some weaknesses.

The problems with the form above are as follows:

1. Many users don't know, don't understand, or don't remember the differences between an email address and a URL. ("I use AOL, so I guess they want me to enter *aol.com*.") This may not be true in your world, but believe me, it's true in the rest of the world. The people using your applications are not nearly as computer-savvy as you think (unless, of course, your target audience is composed of other developers).

2. Zip codes come in two forms in the United States: the short form of five digits, and the long form of nine digits. Some forms offer the ability to enter all nine digits. Some don't. Some of those forms require hyphens between the first five digits and last four. Some don't. It's not clear which version can be used in this form.

3. The **I'm Done** button is fairly personable, but it's also enabled by default, which means users can click it to submit the form data at anytime—even when no field has been completed. This will produce errors. The goal is to avoid errors (more on this in Chapter 6).

4. Nothing indicates which fields are required. This can result in error messages if some fields are, in fact, required. At the very least, users have to wonder whether or not fields are required because so many other forms have required fields. The expectation is to find some sort of indicator.

5. No feedback is given as a result of completing form fields. The user must simply *guess* how to enter data in the correct way.

Time to apply some instructive design.

To fix the first issue—that many users are likely to enter something other than a valid email address—we can provide a default value in the text field. The most useful instructive text in this case is a fake email address because it shows users all the elements of an email address that must be entered. Again, the font color should be a midtone gray instead of the default black.

Another way to hint that the displayed data is instructive rather than already completed is to italicize it. We can do this in the Zip field as well, so users know exactly what version of a zip code can or should be entered. We can also add a simple disclaimer to the form to indicate that all fields are required. And just for good measure, we can add a default value to the State menu to prompt users to choose an item.

Applying instructive text to the form clears up a few questions.

Finally, to prevent users from attempting to submit an incomplete form, we can disable the I'm Done button until all required fields are complete.

A disabled button means users can't even attempt to submit form data until everything is just right. Believe it or not, this is a good thing.

This is a vast improvement to the original form, but we can take it much further. To provide real-time feedback to the user that the form is being completed correctly or incorrectly, we can add visual cues to let him know what's going on by performing inline validation on each form element.

To do this, we can display icons when the user clicks or tabs to a new field to let him know the previous field has been correctly completed, and inline error messages to indicate when the field contains data the system can't use.

Inline validation and well-written error messages tell me I've messed up my email address. It also tells me how to enter it correctly.

Here, check-mark icons are shown to let the user know a field has been completed in a way that agrees with the system. As soon as the user leaves a field that is correctly completed, the check-mark icon appears. In the code for the page, JavaScript is used to verify that the Full Name field, for example, has had a string of characters entered into it. If not, an error message is displayed immediately.

Errors are shown in the right place and at the right time: the very second the user makes the mistake and tries to move on. When the user tabs away from the Email address field having entered an invalid email address, a red text message appears directly beneath the form field, so he knows not only that there has been an error, but also which field contains the error.

The key to an effective error message in a form like this is to avoid leaving the user wondering how to fix the problem. Many error messages simply inform the user an error exists. In the image above, however, the error message tells the user what needs to be entered in the field. This prompts him to fix the entry and tells him how to fix it.

Finally, once all required fields in the form have been completed correctly, the I'm Done button is enabled, letting the user know he has done all he needs to do and can move forward.

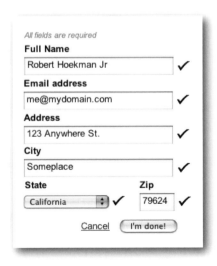

Check marks offer immediate feedback every time I complete a field correctly, motivating me to continue. When all is well, the I'm Done button lights up and I'm on my way. No mistakes. No mess. No questions.

Yes, this version of the form is more visually complex than before, and yes, the form is more difficult to build than the original (building a form this way requires DHTML), but inline validation and instructive text help keep the user confident that he will complete the interaction correctly and continue being productive.

Incidentally, since the **I'm Done** button is disabled until the required fields are completed, it's actually now impossible to submit the form data until it's correct, so the user will never find himself in a situation where he feels false hope that the form is complete, and he will not see a refreshed page with error messages displayed. (We'll talk at length about handling errors in Chapter 6.)

Instructive design, applied in forms or otherwise, helps beginners learn how to complete an interaction and simply serves as a reminder to intermediate and expert users without getting in their way.

▶ Choose Good Defaults

Many Web applications offer configuration options at every turn. This usually happens because developers like to offer every available option they can to users even if it makes little or no sense to do so. "If it can be done, it shall be offered as an option," they say. But the better way to go is to choose good defaults, because it improves a user's chances of learning an application quickly and allows her to dive in and start exploring without having to make a bunch of decisions all the time.

Users typically don't want to configure applications and customize them as much as developers would like to believe. In fact, most users stick to whatever defaults they are offered and avoid customizing at all. Choosing good defaults, then, is not only important, it means that the decisions we make while developing new applications are decisions we make for all of our users. Defaults have long-lasting effects, and we must be careful about what we put in front of users by default, as the user's first impression (and all the others after that) is greatly affected by what we decide to show them.

Jakob Nielsen, renowned guru of Web usability, says in "The Power of Defaults" (one of his many revered Alertbox articles):

> Users rely on defaults in many other areas of user interface design. For example, they rarely utilize fancy customization features, making it important to optimize the default user experience, since that's what most users stick to.

Doesn't get much simpler than that. Yes, we could try to gather statistics so we have a hard and fast rule to live by, but users don't work that way. The best we can do is use our best judgment and choose good defaults whenever we can in the interest of providing a quality user experience.

Nielsen states in the same article:

> System-provided default values constitute a shortcut since it is faster to recognize a default and accept it than to specify a value or an option. In many cases, users do not even need to see the default value, which can remain hidden on an optional screen that is only accessed in the rare case where it needs to be changed. Defaults also help novice users learn the system since they reduce the number of actions users need to make before using the system, and since the default values give an indication of the kind of values that can be legally specified.

Fortunately, many good defaults are built into applications already and can be used as a lesson in how to choose them. Yahoo email doesn't ask if you want to use regular text or bold text every time you start a new message. Google doesn't ask if you'd like to run a Boolean search or a keyword search. And Amazon doesn't ask if you'd like to see its recommendations based on your previous purchases. These are default behaviors, and obviously they're quite helpful.

A good default is one that is most likely to benefit the most people. While there may be options that can be configured at every turn in many applications, the default options should be the ones users would most likely choose if they had to make the choice.

Consider a help system that includes a search box designed to let users search either the help system or the Web, with radio buttons that let them make the choice. Which option should be selected by default? My vote goes for searching the help system. Odds are the user is there to read help articles, so let's show him help articles.

Consider, too, a site-builder tool like Google Page Creator. First, it automatically selects a template for you so you can immediately start designing. Each template also has a default layout, so if you switch templates, you don't have to make another choice at the same time. You can just start building a page. (If you want to change layouts later on, you can do so without damaging the work you've done in the original layout.) Default fonts and font sizes are used for headings, subheadings, and body text. When you import images, default dimensions are chosen (which you can immediately change via the inline toolbar). Filenames are also assigned by default based on the name you choose as a heading for a page.

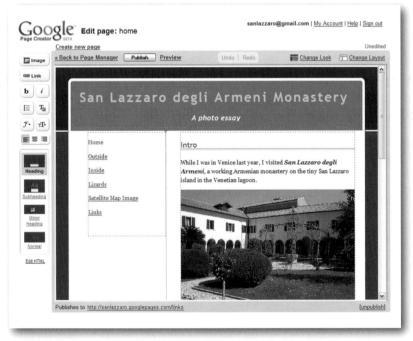

Google Page Creator makes one decision after another for me, so I'm free to be productive instead of being forced to make decisions at every step.

See how many times I said "default" in the preceding paragraph? Sure, you can change anything you want, but defaults get you moving. *Fast.*

Many developers latch onto the idea that users should have every option available to them. But people don't work like that. We'd rather get something done efficiently so we can move on to something else. Decisions get in the way. Options, settings, choices—they all get in the way. For software to be most effective, it needs to get *out* of the way. Choosing good defaults accomplishes this goal.

Integrate preferences

The real goal behind choosing good defaults is not necessarily to get rid of settings and options completely, but to show logical settings by default while still offering alternative settings when they're needed. When this is done well, we can make things even easier by integrating the settings users will likely want to change into the main application screens.

Settings are often best presented in the context of the application itself. Instead of relegating them to a settings screen full of options where users cannot readily see how a setting affects the application, settings can be integrated seamlessly into main application screens and handled inline. For example, default options that can be changed can be shown alongside a **Change This** link that reveals a way to change the setting without leaving the page via an inline form or other widget.

Browsers have evolved enough that they now are usually capable of handling desktop-style interactions. With DHTML (JavaScript, CSS, and HTML), and support for the XMLHTTPRequest object (the core of Ajax, or Asynchronous JavaScript and XML, used to retrieve new data on the fly), chunks of code can be generated dynamically and inserted into an application screen on demand to display controls not available when a page is first loaded. Leveraging this approach, we can dump functionality and information into a page without directing users to remote administrative screens, and give users a way to change settings without leaving a page or losing context.

By all means, include settings and configurable options if you think people will want them, but don't force users to make decisions at every step. Make decisions for them—long before they ever see the application—that help them get up to speed. If they want to change things, they will. Just let them get their hands dirty first.

▶ Design for Information

The organization of a Web application's features can be determined in a lot of ways. In simpler tools, the answers usually present themselves. After all, an application with few features really can't hide much, so each feature is often equally as important as the next. But more complex solutions, like intranets and company-wide accounting systems and such, are a different story altogether. In cases like these, we can learn quite a bit from the world of information architecture.

Information architects have been spinning complicated globs of data into works of organizational art for years, and this expertise has carried over to the Web, where it helps keep sites like CNN.com and NYTimes.com on the straight and narrow. From this world of expertise, we can gain incredible insight into how users would organize features if the choice were theirs, and learn how users search for things on the Web.

The Boxes and Arrows article "Four Modes of Seeking Information and How to Design for Them" (**www.boxesandarrows.com/view/four_modes_of_seeking_ information_and_how_to_design_for_them**), written by Donna Maurer, discusses four principle ways that users search for content within information-based Web sites. The four methods Maurer talks about are:

1. **Known item.** In this search method, users know what they're looking for and know the words they need to look for to stay on the trail. Typical support methods for this type of information-seeking are navigation, indexes, and search features.

2. **Exploratory.** In exploratory searching, users may know what they're looking for, but may be unable to put it in words in a way that allows them to jump on a trail and start following it. In these cases, presenting related information can be of great help to users, as it increases the odds that they will stumble across the right words and go into known-item mode.

3. **Don't know what you need to know.** This mode of seeking is employed by users who may think they need to find one thing, when in fact they need to find something else. Or they may be scavenging the Web for no particular reason, just browsing their way

around to see what comes up. In this mode, short, concise answers that link to deeper explanations can be helpful so users don't waste a lot of time reading through the wrong information.

4. **Re-finding.** This mode becomes important when users are attempting to find something they already found before. One way to address this mode of seeking is to enable users to mark their favorite pages somehow or use the system to remember recent activity.

These four methods certainly encapsulate most of how I find information online. Although the article isn't specific to Web applications, it does provide a useful clue into how users might try to locate operations within a Web application.

Addressing each of these modes is simple enough to achieve, especially now that you know about them. To put this in context of an application, pretend you're designing an application that lets users record podcasts, associate them with a feed users set up themselves, and list the individual shows on their own page within the site.

For known items, when a user knows what she's looking for, logical keywords are generally enough to get her on the right path. A quick way to head her toward recording a new podcast is to use words like *create* and *record* in the main navigation. To help her set information about her feeds so she can better market the podcasts to other people, words like *describe* and *settings* will catch her eye while she scans her account pages. These are **trigger words** that will make it easy for users to find what they need. (We'll talk more about trigger words later in this chapter.)

In another instance, the user might be looking for information on ID3 tags (metadata associated with an audio file), but may not know the term for such information. All he knows is that he wants to provide information about the author of his podcast, the publication date, duration, and other details. In this case, where the user is in exploratory mode, a button labeled **Podcast Details** could provide access to all these things on a single screen.

If the user is looking for information on how to apply a different theme to the podcast player that appears on her page, but doesn't know that the word *theme* is typically how color palettes and font styles are categorized ("don't know what you need to know"), you might avoid using the word *theme* altogether. In this case, surfacing several words all associated with themes will be helpful to newer users who haven't yet made the association.

For example, a menu named Themes can be used as part of the main configuration screen for the podcast player, but a "quick tip" on the page that informs the user she can change the color of her player will lead her to the Themes screen, where she will then learn about themes. Even better, you might show the player on the same page where the user creates his podcast, and simply provide a couple of options to change its appearance, bypassing the Themes screen altogether and keeping the creation process in the context of what other users will see once the activity has been completed.

Finally, a list of recent activities the user has performed or a favorites list could be just the thing for helping the user remember the name of the podcast he listened to last week on another user's page so he can jump straight back to it and send the URL to his friend. This method of enabling the user to "re-find" information will make the information-seeking task effortless. And without even realizing what makes your application so great, the user will be on his way in seconds flat, happy as a clam that he found what he needed without a lot of trouble.

There are almost certainly more than four modes of seeking information (for example, knowing what you're looking for, but having no idea where to look), but these four provide an excellent base. Providing for these four modes alone should keep us all busy for a while.

Card sorting

Card-sorting exercises can be a great way to learn how users think things should be organized within an application. Typically used by information architects to help determine an understandable navigation scheme within an information space, like a Web site, card sorting can help us organize application features just as well by revealing to us what trigger words our users associate with the types of features we plan to include.

Card sorting for applications starts with a simple stack of index cards. The idea is to write down all the features you plan to build, hand the stack off to some appropriate users, and ask them to sort the cards into stacks according to how they think the features should be organized. The exercise is very simple to perform, produces results quickly, and is inexpensive, so it's a viable option for any company looking to solve an information design problem quickly.

The first step in performing a card-sorting exercise is, obviously, to determine the list of things that need to be sorted. And while this may be a simple enough task, as it's a quick matter of writing down the names of each of the features on separate index cards, it's important to keep the stack of cards down to a reasonable size so participants in the card-sorting session don't get overwhelmed by the sheer volume of things to organize. If your application has a lot of features, try to organize some of them on your own, or split the work into two sessions so each group can take on a smaller set.

Also, while writing down features on the cards, avoid using keywords in the feature or operation names that imply an organization, like "Insert table" coupled with "Insert form." It will be far too easy for participants to latch onto the term *insert* and name a menu by that name even if it's not the most appropriate. And avoid using terms that might end up being used as menu, panel, or toolbar names. The whole point of the exercise is to see how users group the features.

Participants in the session should be people who will actually use the application once it's built, as this will help ensure the right people are doing the organizing. This group should be kept small so it doesn't become too difficult for you to keep the session focused on moving forward.

During the session, the only real goal is to get the participants to organize the cards in whatever way they see fit. To facilitate this, the session should begin with a quick explanation of what they'll be doing. Hand them the stack of cards, set down a second stack of blank cards, and instruct the participants to sort the cards into stacks of related groups and write down a name for each group on one of the blank cards.

Your goal as mediator is to keep things moving forward. If the group gets stuck on a certain card or debates at length how to name a certain stack, encourage everyone to move the unnamed cards to a separate stack to be sorted later. Simply flip the proverbial coin to choose possible names for card stacks that don't immediately beg specific names, and write them down as title cards instead of fixating. It's not important that every last detail is worked out, only that some initial impressions are made so you can better determine how users in your target audience associate the different features and operations within the application.

It's important as well to take notes during the session. Try to record the suggestions and confusing points that emerge from discussion during the card sort. These, along with the final stacks of sorted cards, will help you determine how to name and group all kinds of things in your application. Menus and toolbars, for example, can easily be organized according to how users in the session think they go together.

When all the cards have been sorted, thank everyone for their time and take the stacks back to your desk to start sorting out the details.

Yes, that was a very bad pun. Sorry about that.

One thing to note here is that if your application has multiple types of users, each using the application in a different way, you should consider holding card-sorting sessions with groups of users from each type. By doing this you can compare the differences and decide how to accommodate each of the groups in your design.

For more information about card sorting, check out James Robertson's very thorough article "Information Design Using Card Sorting" at **www.steptwo. com.au/papers/cardsorting**. It's aimed primarily at more typical information architectures, like that of a Web site focused on information rather than interaction, but knowledge you gain from the article can certainly be applied to application design as well.

▶ Stop Getting Up to Speed and Speed Things Up

Once beginners become intermediates, they don't want to keep tripping over up-to-speed aids. Not all the tools that help get people moving forward need to stick around for the long haul. Beginner tools can actually interfere with intermediate users in the long run by making them feel disrespected. They're not beginners anymore, so it's time to stop getting users up to speed and start speeding things up.

First, we can get rid of the up-to-speed aids. Welcome screens, for example, in addition to providing an option to be hidden, can be designed with rules about how and when they appear. For a relatively simple application intended for frequent use, for example, a welcome screen can be set to disappear automatically after the user has logged in and used the application a few times. This is roughly equivalent to telling a friend you've taught him everything he needs to know and he should try to fly on his own for a while. (Of course, there should be an easy way to get the screen back should the user feel a little lost without it.) Once a user is comfortable with an application, the welcome screen becomes an obstacle that gets in the way of other, more important features, but strangely, odds are the user won't even notice it's gone.

Blank-slate filler help should also disappear. In most cases, a blank slate doesn't stay blank for long, so your filler might only show up for a few minutes, if even that long, as a user learns what to do in the application. But hey, if it helped a user get moving, it's done its job. Time to go.

Once some of these aids are out of the way, we can also do some small things to speed up task completion for users.

Making software adapt to users is not always the simplest thing to do, but it's well worth it. An application that seems to get smarter the more a user interacts with it stands a good chance of making her even more pleased with the tool as she goes along.

For example, continuing with the example of a stock photography site from earlier chapters, the image library the user builds up while browsing through thousands of images can feature a way to categorize the images he adds to the library. After he has created categories and decides to add a new image to the library, a menu can be offered that enables him to assign the image to a category he's already created. This menu can be set to remain hidden until categories have been created. It can also assign images to a General category by default so the user doesn't have to make this decision every time he adds a new image.

A search engine application can offer a way for users to save their searches and run them again on repeat visits. Google does this via its Search History feature and it's definitely a time-saver. Provided you have a Google account (which is free), a **Search History** link appears in the upper-right corner next to the **My Account** link. Any searches you run are stored by Google and presented on the Search History page, which lists your previous searches in order of date, complete with a date-chooser widget so you can filter the list. Simply click the search term to run the search again. This record of your searches is a great way to avoid having to actually remember anything. Isn't technology great?

Reuse the welcome screen as a notification system

Not all up-to-speed aids have to go away permanently once a user is comfortable with an application. After users can move fluidly through your application, those old sacrificial lambs can come out to play once in a while with a new purpose.

A welcome screen, for example, can be set to reappear when a new and important feature is added to the interface, so users are guided toward its use and shown how to get started with it. In this way, welcome screens can be reused as a notification system for new features and anything else that comes up that might be really important.

Blank-slate fillers can also return anytime a user's page is emptied out (hopefully not as a result of some serious damage to a database on your part).

The bookmark manager Dashboard HQ (described earlier) does this whenever a user's page is void of content. If the user has no bookmark lists or other content displayed, a screen shot of a sample page is shown, and the Add Content pane is opened by default so users can again start adding new content to the page.

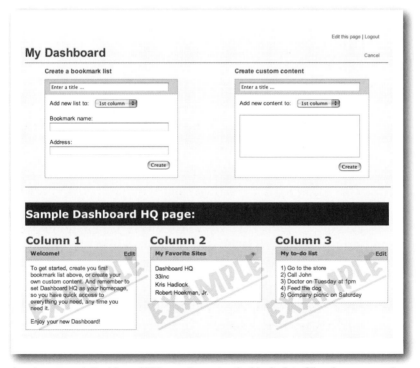

Anytime a user's Dashboard HQ page is empty, the blank-slate filler shows examples of the types of content users can add to it.

Dashboard HQ's blank-slate filler initially shows up for new users who have not yet had a chance to add content to the page, but we figure that if an existing user has no content, he's probably not visited the page in quite a while after having removed all the previous content, and might need a reminder about what he can do with his page, so we show the screen shot again.

(You can learn more about Dashboard HQ at **www.dashboardhq.com**.)

Use one-click interfaces

Amazon does something that really helps users get things done quickly. It provides a patented one-click system that enables users who have already stored their billing and shipping information with a way to make a purchase in a single click.

Amazon's mystical, magical one-click button. So easy it's crazy to switch to another online bookseller.

Clearly, this works to Amazon's advantage. First, it makes it really simple for repeat customers to buy more stuff. Second, it increases what is known as the "cost of switching." That is, the cost of switching to another online bookseller is slightly higher as a result of having such an easy way to purchase items. Users moving to a new bookseller have to create new accounts and enter all the billing and shipping info from scratch. Later on, users will likely have to continue entering the information with every purchase, because Amazon is the only one with the one-click system.

Amazon's system is patented, but nothing says we can't apply similar techniques to our own interfaces. We can at least get it down to two clicks.

One to click through to the shipping cart, where the user is shown the billing information he has stored currently, and the second click to make the purchase.

Amazon even extends this functionality to email campaigns. Recently, I received an email advertisement from Amazon about a specific book—not a list of books, just one—that was related to a topic I searched through a couple of weeks or so ago. The email told me about the book and offered a button by which I could purchase it. I clicked the button. The purchase was so easy that I completely forgot about it until just a few minutes ago when I received another email to let me know the book has been shipped. Not only was the purchase process made faster, it was catered entirely to me because Amazon knows what I want based on my prior visits and adapts what it sends to my in-box to show me things I'll likely want to buy. Amazon really has this efficiency thing down pat. You can bet I won't be switching to another bookseller any time soon.

Google Page Creator offers a smart way to speed things up as well. Once the user has chosen a template and layout for her site, any new page she creates uses the same template. Users are not forced to remember which template they chose previously. They are simply given what is most likely to be the template they would choose if the choice was offered. Users can, of course, use a different template for each page if they so choose, but since this is not likely to be desired, Google makes a smart decision for the user and gives her the same template. This little technique promotes good practices (it's good for a site to maintain a consistent look and feel) and makes it very easy for users to generate quality work.

Use design patterns to make things familiar

A big part of what makes an obvious design is the element of familiarity. When we learn how one application works, we can quickly apply what we've learned when working with other applications.

Google, Yahoo, and MSN all handle pagination in search results pages with the same type of interaction. Each one features a series of links (in the form of page numbers) for jumping from one page to the next, and each includes a **Next** link for walking through the search results in a linear path. This is a design pattern.

Expanding this definition, design patterns are common solutions to common problems. In the case of search engines, pagination is a common issue in the various applications. Each chose to use the same pattern—the pagination pattern—but each chose to do it a little differently from the others.

Patterns are frameworks for designs, not specific rules, so they leave a lot of room for creativity and innovation (innovation, in fact, is often an extension of existing patterns). Each search engine uses page numbers as links, and each one includes a **Next** link, but each looks different from the others. They don't actually need to look the same. It's only important that each user who visits each site can quickly understand how it handles navigation through multiple pages of search results. Since the pagination functionality is so effective, many sites have implemented their own variations on the design, elevating it to the status of design pattern.

In My Yahoo, the design patterns used to handle all of the editing within a page were unfamiliar to me at first, but since signing up, the patterns have appeared in a number of Web applications, and I've been able to move from one to the other with little effort because each one is leveraging the experiences I've had with previous applications. This familiarity makes new applications easier to learn, explore, and master.

Design patterns tend to emerge when the pattern in question proves itself to be effective over time. When it works on one site, others emulate it, and when it succeeds across many sites, everyone else starts to use the design. Before you know it, the pattern can be seen all over the Web.

Design patterns help users learn new applications quickly by allowing them to parlay their previous experience from other sites to the new application, and for this reason, patterns can be immensely helpful when attempting to design the obvious.

The major lesson to learn here is that when you're designing a new application, you should pay attention to what patterns are used by similar or related applications and try to leverage them in your own. The growing use of these patterns will tear down many of the barriers users face when trying to learn a new application, allowing them to learn yours more quickly.

This book is not about design patterns—it's more about the conceptual, application-level patterns that make Web software great—but there is a book all about design patterns called *Designing Interfaces,* by Jennifer Tidwell, that can provide a wonderful base of information about patterns and serve as an ongoing reference for when you get stuck on a design problem and need a good standard to rely on. I highly recommend you check it out. You know, after you finish up *Designing the Obvious.*

▶ Provide Help Documents, Because Help Is for Experts

Jensen Harris, who works on the Microsoft Office team, once talked on his blog about how infrequently users access help documentation (this post is available at **blogs.msdn.com/jensenh/archive/2005/11/29/497861.aspx**). Instead of jumping to the help files any time a user needs to understand something new, he'll attempt to learn the procedure himself. As counterintuitive as it may be, expert users are actually the ones most likely to check help files.

My own usability testing experiences confirm this. It's extremely rare for a new or intermediate user to dig through or even seek out the provided help documentation. (It's actually pretty shocking how infrequently users rely on help documents. A recent usability session on a fairly complicated application, where users were in constant need of assistance, showed that not one of the five testers looked for help articles. One of them even said she wished help was available, but never looked for it, despite the fact that a link to it was prominently displayed in the main interface.)

Harris tries to explain this in the context of his own history. When he made the move to the Office team, he immediately went to a bookstore to buy a book on Excel to increase his skills instead of relying on help documentation.

He believes this lack of interest in help is the result of several factors. First, there is a language barrier in help documentation. Users may be in exploratory mode, but they likely won't know the terminology they need to locate the right information. Most help systems don't produce search results nearly as well as Google, and users are often limited to using exact terminology and feature names to find what they need. This doesn't work when you're new to an application, and often fails even if you're an intermediate user. Experts, on the other hand, know the lingo used by an application and can quickly find specific information within a help system.

Second, help documentation generally lacks the personality usually found in books and articles on the same subjects. Help files are meant to be technically accurate and concise, but authors of books and articles can loosen up and inject humor and liveliness into a piece to bring the material to life in a way help files usually cannot.

Finally, the Web itself is one of the greatest help resources around, and many people latch onto it because the *voice* found there is more appealing. Online articles, forum posts, and blogs full of information on features and examples are as easy to find as a simple search through Google. These authors are not held back by the same constraints most tech writers face, so the information found there can be of greater use, as it's easier to digest information wrapped in a friendly package.

For these reasons, the more effective approach to teaching new users how to move around in your application is to apply the techniques outlined earlier in this chapter. But when you do get some expert users, help documentation can be the perfect thing to keep them happy and motivated to learn more.

Backpack provides a nice example of how help documentation can be done well. First, it doesn't focus on terminology exclusive to the application. (This is true mainly because the application itself is so simple and easy to understand.) Second, it is written with a personal tone and reads as if it's a tech-savvy friend standing over your shoulder answering questions. An added bonus is that the help documentation is entirely contained in—you guessed it—a Backpack page, which means it stays in context, and thus continues displaying the list of Backpack pages you created so you can immediately jump back into the application. Putting users at ease like this lowers the perceived learning curve and answers questions without a lot of hassle.

Box.net does something similar. Instead of providing an elaborate help system that requires a relatively deep understanding of the software, it offers a single-screen help page. The right side of the page features a simple vertical navigation bar made up of all the available topics. Just click and read!

Box.net offers a box full of help content in this single-screen interface that serves up content without a single page refresh.

While applications should really be designed for intermediate users, it's important to keep experts happy as well, for they are the people who have invested the most time and energy into learning and using our applications. To this end, a little well-designed and well-written help can go a long way.

6

Handle Errors Wisely

When I use a Web application, I want things to go smoothly. I don't want intrusive errors popping up to tell me I did something that the system can't handle. I don't want to be interrupted. I don't want to know the system doesn't work. And I definitely don't want to be blamed for its shortcomings by an error message that tells me I did something wrong.

Our users don't want these things either.

When we perform a task in an application that results in an error message, we blame ourselves. After all, we're the ones not smart enough to use the application correctly. We don't understand what it is *we're* supposed to do, and that's why *we're* doing it wrong.

But somehow, because we're computer-savvy, when we find out that *other* people using an application *we* built are having problems, we think those people are just too dumb to use it. We blame them. After all, they're the ones not smart enough to use the application correctly. They don't understand what it is *they're* supposed to do, and that's why *they're* doing it wrong.

Clearly, there's a problem with our logic.

Because I spend all my time designing Web applications, and because I don't want to perpetuate these obnoxious error messages and make *my* users feel stupid, I've spent quite a bit of time considering how errors are displayed, what causes them, and when they are shown. Through this, I've managed to come up with one fairly obvious conclusion:

The best way to handle errors is to prevent them from ever occurring.

When an application is bad, it's bad for a thousand different reasons. When it's good, it's good because the user is able to glide through each and every interaction effortlessly, without hassle and without being forced to learn how the underlying system works to accomplish the user's goals.

To rise to this seemingly unreachable level of quality, we need to handle errors before and after they occur. The goal is not to tell the user something has gone wrong. The goal is to design the system in such a way that the user never has a chance to make a mistake. And if a mistake does occur, we need to make it as painless as possible to get back on track quickly.

There are plenty of places mistakes can be made. Good design can cure most of them.

▶ Prevent and Catch Errors with Poka-yoke Devices

Poka-yoke devices are all around us.

Poka-yoke (pronounced *POH-kah YOH-kay*) is the Japanese term for "mistake-proofing." A poka-yoke *device* is whatever is used to prevent an error. It's what makes something foolproof.

The Popcorn button on a microwave oven is a poka-yoke device. Stick the popcorn in, push the button, and watch the microwave turn a bag full of little seeds into a night in front of a good movie. No thought required.

The remote for my car locks all the doors at once, so I don't have to wonder if I left any unlocked. My car has a little plastic strap that tethers the gas cap to the car, so I won't accidentally leave it on my trunk and drive off without it properly attached. The keys can't be removed from the ignition unless the engine has been turned off. And I can't put the transmission in reverse unless I'm at a complete stop.

Dryers stop running when the door is opened so no one gets hurt. Irons shut off automatically after sitting idle for a while to help prevent fires. The bathroom sink has a small hole toward the top of the rim that prevents the sink from overflowing.

Poka-yoke devices are *everywhere*.

Sadly, they don't show up on the Web nearly as often as they should. When they do, though, it's fantastic. Users can get things done without incident. Things go smoothly. You know, the way things *should* go.

Poka-yoke on the Web

A Web-mail application I use a lot has a built-in memory of what I do with specific kinds of email messages.

For example, every time I got an email from my task-management system that said "Status changed" in the subject line (the email is sent whenever I change the details of a task), I would throw it away by checking the check box next to the subject line, choosing the Trash option from a drop-down menu, and then clicking the <u>Move</u> button. After the first time I did this, however, I noticed that I no longer had to choose Trash from the drop-down menu. After checkmarking a message I wanted to throw away, I noticed the Trash option was being automatically selected for me. All I had to do was click <u>Move</u> to throw the email away.

The people who built the application did this on purpose. They figured that since it's statistically probable I will move a message to the same place I moved all the other ones that were just like it (which all had "Status changed" in the subject line and were sent from the same email address), the application, very politely, remembers that I have thrown all the other messages into the Trash and selects that option *for* me in the drop-down menu.

It's the tiniest detail, but it prevents me from making the common mistake of moving items to the wrong folder. (It also makes me feel as if the application is reading my mind, which is a little creepy, but that's a different story.)

Let's face it. Most of what's really bad about an application is how many times we mess something up while trying to use it. Good design can cure this. So implementing poka-yoke devices is probably the number one thing you can do to improve your user's experience. Even the worst designs can be improved by eliminating the possibility of errors.

Prevention devices

There are two types of poka-yoke devices: prevention devices and detection devices.

Prevention devices are those that prevent errors from ever occurring. The hole in the rim of the sink that keeps it from overflowing is a prevention device. The user can leave the water running all he wants to—the sink will never overflow.

Keeping users from making mistakes on the Web is no small task, but there are plenty of things that can be done to minimize most of the potential errors and keep users feeling productive.

Problems are big, fixes are small

When we were creating Dashboard HQ, the initial design went through several small iterations. At one time, the Add Content pane was designed so that the user had to choose which column a new module would go into once it was created. It was easy to forget to choose a column number from the menu prior to creating the module, so we considered what type of error message would best handle the situation. A red text message that appeared in the pane? A little box at the top of the page that faded in to catch the user's eye and tell him what went wrong?

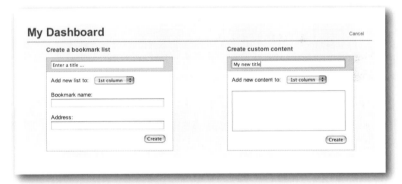

Dashboard HQ makes it impossible to mess up when adding new content.

We quickly realized the best way to take care of the issue was to make it impossible to make the mistake. In true poka-yoke fashion, we simply set "1st column" as the default value, making it impossible to produce the situation that required the error message. Not only was this method foolproof, it also meant we could improve the application substantially without writing a single new line of code. In this case, the poka-yoke prevention device was a single attribute inside of a single HTML element. Five seconds later, it was done.

But we didn't stop there. Next, we removed the code that checked for values in the fields the user should fill out to create a new module. In truth, it isn't necessary for a module to have something in it to exist. It can simply exist. It can just sit somewhere on the page with a default title ("Enter a title...") and no content whatsoever. Users can always edit the module after it is created—in fact, that's the whole point of the application—so why stop them from creating it?

In just a few minutes of modifying and testing, we completely erased the potential to make a mistake when creating a new module. Users don't need to name the module, add content to it, or choose where it should appear; they can simply open the Add Content pane and click **Create**. There is no way for them to go wrong.

Not only did we avoid having to write more code, we actually *removed* code. In doing this, we also kept ourselves from having to debug the error code (which is always an exercise in irony). One less thing to maintain later on. One less potential problem for users. Win-win.

Remove the possibility of error

Another thing we did for Dashboard HQ was to write a tiny bit of JavaScript that ensures URLs entered into bookmark lists function correctly after being saved. Upon saving a new bookmark, the entered URL is checked to see if http:// was entered at the beginning of the address. If it wasn't, it is added automatically before the bookmark is saved. If a user enters *amazon.com*, for example, the bookmark address is converted to http://amazon.com/.

This script ensures that links work properly in all browsers and that the user is far less likely to see an error after clicking the link later. This poka-yoke device required only a couple of lines of code, but saves users from many potential errors.

Traditionally, poka-yoke devices are simple and cheap. If it takes a lot of work to implement one, you should review the source of the issue to see how you can simplify. Sure, it may mean admitting you were wrong about how your application should work to begin with, but after solving the issue, the application will be leaner and less problematic. (Incidentally, when you accomplish this, it's suddenly easy to admit you were wrong, because it's the precursor to boasting about how gracefully you fixed the problem.)

Many problems can be solved without a lot of extra work. Tiny modifications, like choosing a good default value instead of writing error code to tell users they've done something wrong, are quite often all it takes to improve an application, or even a single interaction, tenfold.

The only downside to using poka-yoke devices is that no one will ever realize how clever we were in coming up with them. The user will never see the error that could have happened. He'll point to his own common sense as the reason he can use the application effectively.

But nothing says we can't smile knowingly from the back row.

Detection devices

In our original design for Dashboard HQ, we were going to write code to show the error to the user immediately so he could fix it and move on. This would have been a detection device. In the case above, we chose the more optimal prevention device, but it's not always possible to prevent every error. When things go wrong—and they will—it's time to rely on the other form of poka-yoke devices, *detection devices*.

When poka-yoke can't be used to prevent an error, it can still be used to detect the error and notify the user so it can be remedied immediately. In Web terms, this usually comes in the form of an error message.

We've all come across a billion error messages (give or take) in the time we've spent using computers, and we've been trained over time to ignore them (unless they look unusual in some way and happen to catch our attention). Just click **OK**, we think, and move on. Oh, wait. Was that something important?

Most of the error messages we see are useless. They are written in cryptic developer-speak, tell us something we already know, don't tell us what to do to remedy the error, and don't offer any choices. If clicking **OK** is the only thing that can be done, we click **OK**. Then we're back at square one. Gee, thanks for the helping hand.

Quality error pages

Most server setups allow the configuration of custom error pages, but many designers neglect this part of an application. And that's a drag, because error pages can do so much to help users that we're really missing an opportunity by ignoring them. Instead of simply telling users a page cannot be found, we can create error pages that guide users straight to other content so they can get moving again without even thinking about the fact that they just saw an error message.

One of my favorite examples of a bad error page is from an old version of the Federal Emergency Management Agency (FEMA) Web site. FEMA has a disaster assistance program for people who have been the victims of some sort of natural disaster, such as a hurricane. At one time, the online application process for this program contained several key problems.

The process began with an image verification system that displayed highly illegible images of words, which users are meant to type in a text field to verify they are human beings and not automated systems. Users were given three chances to enter the correct word. Upon failing the third time, the resulting error message read:

"We are sorry for not being able to proceed your requests because you have failed our tests."

Not only was this message poorly written (for starters, the word *proceed* should have been the word *process*), making it more difficult to understand than it needed to be, but it also offered no way out. There was no link back to the home page, no suggestions about what to do next, nothing. Just a meaningless error message.

And if you were unlucky enough to have had your home wiped out and unlucky enough to have access only to a Macintosh (and this is one of the few times you would be unlucky to have access to a Mac), you would come across another error message informing you that Microsoft Internet Explorer 6 was required to complete the form.

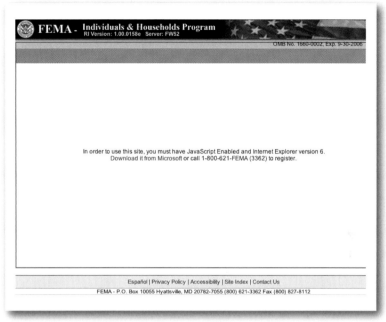

I'm sorry—you want me to download *what* now?

Internet Explorer 6 doesn't exist on Mac. And according to Microsoft, it never will. Users who didn't know this fact were likely to wander off to try to download and install the software equivalent of a purple squirrel.

The worst part is that the browser incompatibility message didn't appear until after the user managed to get past the image verification system. This message did suggest to users that they call FEMA directly or download the appropriate version of Internet Explorer, but the application should have worked in any browser, on any operating system. (At the very least, it should have told users to download a browser that *actually existed*.)

What's so hard, after all, about a simple HTML-based form? Forms are all over the Web. Macintosh users use online forms on a daily basis to purchase books and music, sign up for new Web applications, install software, check email, and so on, with as little effort as any Windows user. How is it that FEMA managed to make something so simple so complex? How is it that they managed to break something that works so well on a million other sites?

Many error pages lack the elements that can help users get moving again, and this is where they fail. Many just explain that the page cannot be found and that the user should hit the **Back** button or head back to the home page and try to find the information another way. This information often comes in the form of bulleted lists that are heavy on text and light on links, and nothing really useful stands out on the page except for the large error message. But the error message is the least helpful part of the page.

Error pages should help users get back on track by offering up links to other pages that do, in fact, exist. Beyond that, they can offer search boxes so users can try to find the missing content another way, continue displaying persistent navigation items so users can jump to the main pages within an application, and even serve up a log-in screen in cases where users have accounts.

All of these things turn what would otherwise be a useless error page into a poka-yoke detection device. They show users that something has gone wrong and immediately offer them a way out. They enable us to create error pages that offer solutions instead of more problems.

Inline validation

Inline validation scripts are one of the best forms of poka-yoke detection devices on the Web, because they catch errors immediately.

Inline validation, handled by JavaScript within a page, is the act of performing real-time checking to verify that an interaction has been completed correctly. In a registration form, for example, inline validation can be used to verify that the user's chosen user name has not already been taken, the email address has been written in the correct format, and the first and last names have been entered. Upon determining that a field value has been incorrectly entered or has been skipped, error messages can be shown *within the form,* before the user ever has the opportunity to click the button that submits the form data.

Our Property (**www.ourproperty.co.uk**), a site that tracks the current costs of buying a home in Europe, has the single best example I've seen of well-designed inline validation.

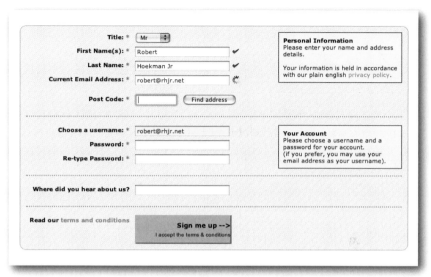

The check marks tell me I'm smart enough to use this application.

Upon entering correct values (or at least the correct type of value), a green check-mark icon displays next to the completed field. When the email address is entered, a loading animation plays while it's validated to ensure the email address is real.

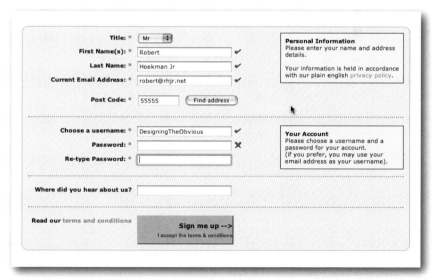

I skipped a required field, but the application told me immediately so I could recover gracefully.

And when a field is skipped, a red X appears to indicate the field was not completed correctly.

These simple interface elements guide users toward a successful interaction. The only thing I would suggest to improve the interaction is to disable the <u>Sign Me Up</u> button until the required fields are complete.

It's important that inline validation be carefully designed so it comes across well. Remember the Milk (**www.rememberthemilk.com**), a to-do list management application, uses inline validation on its registration form, and does a great job of validating that a user name has not already been taken, but error messages are displayed every time a field gains focus, even when the user hasn't yet had time to enter anything into the field. The result is that users are shown error messages almost constantly while completing the form.

Remember the Milk showed me an error message before I even had a chance to make a mistake.

Validation should only be performed when a user leaves or passes over a field that is required without correctly completing it. When a text field that accepts required information, for example, loses focus, an error should be shown. An error should not be shown if the user has not yet had a chance to enter the correct information.

Turn errors into opportunities

Poka-yoke detection devices usually result in the error messages we're all used to seeing—JavaScript alerts and such—but some companies try to improve on this idiom by putting a positive spin on an otherwise negative situation. This is by far one of the best ways to deal with errors that can't be prevented.

For example, when a user's search on Squidoo produces no results, Squidoo turns the error into an opportunity by displaying a message that prompts the user to create a lens on the searched topic.

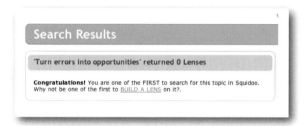

I'm one of the first to search for this topic? Fantastic! I'll build a lens and be a Squidoo pioneer!

Squidoo developers recognized that it takes a lot of time to build up a knowledge base of every subject for which users could possibly search, and attempted to find a way to compel users to create more lenses. Smart move. The poka-yoke device in this case is the search engine itself, detecting that no results are available for a topic and displaying a call to action instead of an error message. The result doesn't even look like an error. It's way too friendly to make a user feel like he's messed up. Instead, the user takes a moment to decide whether or not to create a lens on the subject, which is exactly what Squidoo wants to happen.

Google puts this technique to work as well. When a user runs a search that appears to contain a misspelled word, the first item in the search-results listing is an attempt to clarify what the user was trying to search. (Of course, what actually happens on the Google side to detect misspelled words and suggest alternate spellings is much more complicated, I'm sure, but my mental model is that it *just knows* I misspelled a word.)

Yes, actually—that's exactly what I meant. Thanks! Click.

Google Suggest (labs.google.com/suggest), on the other hand, blurs the line between the two types of poka-yoke devices by putting both to good use. It *detects* what the user is attempting to search so it can keep potential mistakes from occurring, and then *prevents* them by helping the user enter the correct search terms before the search is run. When the user begins entering search terms, a list of words and terms that are likely to match what the user is looking for appears, so the user can choose the desired search term and avoid common misspellings.

Google Suggest helps me spell correctly, type faster, and find common search terms, all without making a single mistake. Nice.

An example from home

I use poka-yoke on my own site as well, to ensure users can properly use the Adobe Flash plug-in to view the content of an eReader application I created to highlight some bits of interface design advice I call "The Web Command-ments" (**www.rhjr.net/eReader**). When a user comes to the page with a ver-sion of the Flash plug-in installed that is older than the version required for the eReader application, error-handling code kicks in to manage the entire experi-ence of upgrading the plug-in version and viewing the content.

The alternate Flash content helps users get started with the upgrade process.

First, the page detects the version of the Flash plug-in installed in the user's browser. If an old version is found, in place of the eReader application an alter-nate Flash (.swf) file is loaded that prompts the user to upgrade the plug-in. If the user proceeds with the installation, her browser is reopened automatically (in some browsers) to the same page once the installation is complete and she is shown the eReader application. If the user cancels the installation or it fails for some reason, the alternate Flash content offers links to other areas of the site so she can move on, as well as a way to retry the installation.

If no Flash plug-in is present (or the version of the plug-in is old enough that the alternate .swf file won't display), alternate content is shown that lets her know what went wrong, tells her how to get the plug-in (along with an image of the content she would be seeing if the plug-in was installed so she knows what she's missing), and offers links to other areas of the site in case she doesn't want to bother with the installation.

When JavaScript is disabled, users are offered a link to the blog and a note asking them to enable JavaScript.

If JavaScript, which is required to run the version detection scripts, is disabled in the user's browser, she is told that JavaScript is required for the page, and is asked to enable scripting in her browser and refresh the page.

Of course, if nothing goes wrong, the user sees the Web Commandments in all their glory and never knows about all the processes that took place to ensure the content would be shown.

Finally, the **About the Web Commandments** link, which hides and shows (via a toggle function) an area of the page used to display the description of the document currently loaded into the eReader application, appears only if the eReader application is displayed correctly. If alternate content is being shown, the link is never created. This little magic trick is achieved with the combined use of Flash and JavaScript. The eReader application itself checks the loaded XML file (which contains the text and image references for the Web Commandments content) for a description element. If the description is found, it is parsed by the eReader application and passed to a JavaScript in the page.

JavaScript enabled? Check. Correct version of the Flash plug-in? Check. Show the content!

The <u>About the Web Commandments</u> link doesn't show up unless the Web Commandments show up first.

The JavaScript, in turn, dynamically writes the HTML it needs to display the description and the **About the Web Commandments** link.

The JavaScript is a poka-yoke device. Without it, if no description was found in the XML file, the link would show and hide an area of the page that was void of content, thereby making the link appear broken. With the JavaScript, users never see a broken link.

The Flash detection procedures that run on the Web Commandments page detect potential issues and offer appropriate error messages that try to get the user back on track. They also prevent a much worse error from occurring by displaying the alternate content. Without this, some users would see a blank, white box (meaning a Flash plug-in is installed, but is too old to display the content) or a rather poorly designed browser prompt that tells the user the plug-in is missing and offers a way to install it. Yes, the browser prompt offers a way to install the plug-in, but at the time of this writing, the dialog box displayed by Internet Explorer to start the installation is labeled "Security Warning." This is not something you want to your users to see. Remember, error pages and messages should help the user move forward. Security warnings are not the way to go.

Feeling smart

Detecting errors and guiding users to deal with them immediately is much less aggravating than waiting until they click a **Submit** button or make a mistake. At that point, it's far too late because the user already has an expectation that the next thing she sees will be whatever comes next in the process. If she is shown a registration form a second time, this time with errors, her expectation will be broken and she may lose confidence in her ability to complete the form correctly the second time. If she searches for something that has no results and sees an error, she can lose confidence in her ability to search well within that particular search engine. If she loses confidence in herself, she's much more prone to stop using your application. Inline validation and other methods of implementing poka-yoke help ensure errors are dealt with before the user's confidence is diminished. Our goal is to make her feel smart. Smart enough to use our application. If we help *her* feel smart, she'll like *us* a whole lot more.

Whenever possible, errors should be prevented instead of detected. The code required to perform inline validation is not always easy to create, but it's far better for the user than tossing up JavaScript alerts and the like after the user has been given hope that things will go smoothly. Displaying errors after this point is, well, too little too late. If the errors cannot be prevented from ever occurring, applications should at least be courteous enough to detect them as they occur so the user always knows exactly what's going on and can remain productive. The application should also make a decent attempt to get the user back on track by spinning the error message as an opportunity rather than an error.

▶ Ditch Anything Modal

Error messages in desktop-installed applications are most often displayed in some sort of modal dialog box. Paraphrasing the Apple Human Interface Guidelines, there are three types of dialog boxes:

Modeless. Enables users to change settings in a dialog while still interacting with document windows; the Find window in many word processors is an example of a modeless dialog. Modeless dialogs have title bar controls (close, minimize, and zoom buttons).

Document-modal. Prevents the user from doing anything else within a particular document. The user can switch to other documents in the application and to other applications.

Application-modal. Prevents the user from doing anything else within the owner application; the user can switch to another application. Most application-modal dialogs do not have the standard title bar controls (close, minimize, zoom); the user dismisses these dialogs by clicking a button, such as OK or Cancel.

Modality exists on the Web as well, but it comes in a slightly different form. Pop-up windows, for example, are modeless. They are often used in applications to configure settings and change preferences (for example, to add or remove a user from a Web-mail program), but they don't interfere with a user's ability to work with the parent window. Sure, clicking the parent window usually means losing track of the pop-up window, whether intentionally or not, but at least you can still interact with the main part of the application.

JavaScript alerts, however, are application-modal. Not only do they prevent the user from interacting with other parts of a Web application, they also hijack the browser itself by making it impossible to switch pages or tabs or close the browser until the user clicks a button in the alert to close it. The user is left with no choice but to deal with the alert. She is unable to move on until the magical **OK** button is clicked.

This behavior is just plain rude. It's not the user's job to jump through every little hoop an application comes up with. It's the job of the software to do what the user wants.

Redesigning rude behavior

Getting rid of application-modal messages in favor of document-modal messages has become an interesting, albeit disturbing, trend on the Web.

Instead of relying on JavaScript alert messages, for example, designers have been creating floating inline dialog boxes that serve the same purpose. It's as though everyone heard that users hate JavaScript alerts and decided they'd cure the issue by moving the confirmation messages and such into the page instead.

In one example I stumbled across recently, a message appeared that *looked* like a JavaScript alert, but it was displayed in the page itself as a floating box, complete with drag behavior. I could drag the error message around all I wanted to, but I couldn't move past it without clicking **OK**. This was a document-modal message. I could still interact with the browser itself, but not the application.

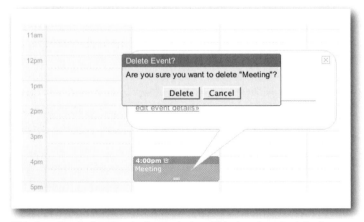

This faux JavaScript alert is disappointing. All it does is a nice job of redesigning rude behavior.

In another case, the entire page was dimmed out and all its interactions were disabled while a modal dialog box displayed in the center of the page. Also document-modal.

Listen up, fellow designers. The issue isn't that the errors come in the form of separate controls, like JavaScript alerts. The issue is that the messages are modal. Making the messages document-modal isn't any better. Yes, document-modal messages still allow the users to interact with the browser or leave the page, but these messages still interrupt workflow, prevent users from working with the rest of an application while dealing with the message, and do so unnecessarily. A new spin on the same old trick is not the answer.

A new design for modal errors doesn't cure the problem. *It just moves it.* These designers are just finding more interesting ways to make the same mistake. They're redesigning rude behavior.

Replace it with modeless assistants

Instead of redesigning rude modal alert messages, we need to devise better solutions that help users maintain forward momentum while using our applications. We can do this by going modeless.

For example, we can implement undo functions instead of relying on implementation-model, application-modal JavaScript alerts or document-modal errors and confirmation messages (especially ones that act like faux JavaScript alerts). Undo functions have been around for a long time in desktop applications, but somehow this behavior wasn't translated for the Web—that is, until Google decided to create undo functions for its popular Web-mail application, Gmail.

When messages are deleted in Gmail, a notification appears toward the top of the page that tells the user the conversation has been moved to the Trash and offers an **Undo** link. As expected, clicking the **Undo** link reinserts the deleted messages back into the list of messages.

I can undo my last operation? Brilliant! Bravo, Google. Bravo.

Google does three things right with this feature.

First, it eliminates the need to show confirmation messages that ask the user if she's sure she wants to throw the messages away.

Second, it offers a way to get the deleted messages back.

Finally, *it shows the user how to do it* via the inline text message at the top of the page.

The message is exposed right when it needs to be, and the yellow background used to display the message draws the eye right to it, so users are much more likely to see the message and know the feature exists. This message remains visible until the user performs a new action, like creating a new message or deleting another conversation. In other words, it stays active just long enough for users to backtrack and undo the delete action.

What Google did was brilliant, but not because implementing an undo feature was an original idea. It was brilliant because no one else was doing it on the Web and it's the right thing to do.

Now that Google has proven undo functions can be created on the Web, and has shown us a great way to do it, we're all out of excuses. Any application that allows users to perform what are normally irreversible actions should include an undo function.

I know, I know, building this functionality isn't always going to be easy, but it will definitely be worth it. And hey, someone's bound to release a JavaScript framework one of these days that makes implementing undo features really simple. (Someone, steal this idea and run with it. Please.)

▶ Write Error Messages That Help Instead of Hurt

Jillions of error messages on the Web are written in cryptic developer-speak. *Jillions*. If you're responsible for writing even one error message in an application, now's the time to pay close attention.

Error messages need to be written by someone who knows how to write.

If this is not you, step away from the keyboard and consider taking a writing class. If you do write well enough that other people can read your email messages to them without crossing their eyes, then stick around. You might be a good person to write error messages. It's not glamorous, but it's necessary.

So what's so hard about writing an error message? Well, it's hard because it needs to be done in a way that avoids demeaning people. Developers tend to write error messages during the development phase of any application so it can be debugged more efficiently. But these types of error messages, unfortunately, often make their way into the released product where they confuse and alienate users on a daily basis.

Instead of writing an error that says "[object] is null" (as though that means anything to a non-developer), for example, explain what's happened in plain English and how to deal with it. Say something that makes sense. Say, "Unfortunately, your request could not be handled. Please try again. If the problem persists, please log out and log back in."

Yes, this message has a lot more words, but it also means a lot more to a user. It tells him something has gone wrong and explains what can be done to move forward.

Error messages that do not provide useful information do not help users. They hurt users.

A poorly written error message is one that explains what is wrong in terms not likely to be understood by the user. Here's an example from a fictitious calendar application, in which a user is trying to schedule an event:

"Operation failed."

Users cannot be expected to understand what this means. They will understand that something went wrong, but many users will not know from a message like this how to react, nor will they understand that they were performing an "operation." Some will try the "operation" again. Some will just give up.

Improving the message is a simple matter of using language more likely to be understood.

"We're sorry, but we could not schedule this event. Please try again."

This version of the message tells the user what to do to get back on track, but still doesn't explain what went wrong in a way that prevents the user from repeating the same mistake.

An effective error message might look like this:

"We're sorry, but this event cannot be saved without a date. Please select a date and save it again."

In this version, the error tells the user what went wrong in plain English and offers instructions about how to remedy the error.

Simple changes like these convert error messages from rude bits of useless information into helpful, explanatory bits of *useful* information.

Interface Surgery: Using the inline-expand design pattern

This episode of Interface Surgery is a simple one, but it covers a little DHTML trick that can be used in any application in about a billion ways. I frequently use it to display error messages in Web applications.

The *inline-expand* design pattern is made possible by a simple DIV in an HTML page that is displayed and/or hidden on demand, via JavaScript, based on user interaction. The first time I ever saw this in action was in Macromedia's Weblog aggregator, prior to Adobe Systems' acquisition of Macromedia. The FAQ (Frequently Asked Questions) section of the site contained the usual, long list of questions. But each one was a simple link; no answers appeared on the page. Wondering what would happen when I clicked, I was happy to see the answer presented inline, right where I needed it. No waiting for a page refresh. No pop-up windows.

What is "Designing the Obvious"?

It's about designing Web-based applications that are so simple to use that users attribute their ability to use them effectively to pure common sense.

What does "inline expand" mean?

"Inline expand" is a design pattern that describes the display of a previously hidden page element as the result of user input. The hidden element is simply inserted into the page in an appropriate area, like immediately below the point where the user clicked, appearing somewhat like magic.

How do you pronounce your last name?

It's pronounced "hook-man". It's Dutch. When a Dutch person says it, you can kinda hear the "e" in the name. It comes out "hoo-ek-man", but in a really pleasant, Dutch sort of way.

Are you some kind of weirdo?

Nope. I just have a strange last name.

Why is the sky blue?

Now you've gone too far.

How long did it take to create this piece of DHTML wizardry?

About 15 minutes.

That's a lot of text. I don't really want to read all that.

A typical FAQ page looks rather crowded. It contains a ton of questions, each separated by an answer. All the blocks of text for the answers make the questions harder to pick out. Sure, the questions are somehow visually distinct from the answers, with either a bold font or a different font color, but this isn't usually enough to make the page as clear as it needs to be. Users are forced to scan long pages full of text to find the particular question they need answered.

To clean up this page, the answers must be stripped out of it.

> What is "Designing the Obvious"?
> What does "inline expand" mean?
> How do you pronounce your last name?
> Are you some kind of weirdo?
> Why is the sky blue?
> How long did it take to create this piece of DHTML wizardry?

A short list of links. Much easier to read.

A single JavaScript function (which toggles the answer between visible and hidden), the conversion of each question into a link, and the addition of an ID attribute to each link in the HTML are all it takes to turn the list of remaining questions into links that display answers "automagically."

> What is "Designing the Obvious"?
> What does "inline expand" mean?
>
> *"Inline expand" is a design pattern that describes the display of a previously hidden page element as the result of user input. The hidden element is simply inserted into the page in an appropriate area, like immediately below the point where the user clicked, appearing somewhat like magic.*
>
> How do you pronounce your last name?
> Are you some kind of weirdo?
> Why is the sky blue?
> How long did it take to create this piece of DHTML wizardry?

One chunk of information at a time, please. Thank you.

The much shorter list of questions is significantly easier for users to scan. Spotting the right question is a simple matter of a quick glance down the page. Upon finding the question the user needs answered, he clicks the link and is shown the answer.

I started using the inline-expand pattern to avoid the use of application-modal error messages and document-modal faux JavaScript alerts, like the one described earlier. Using inline expand, when something goes wrong that I can't otherwise prevent with a poka-yoke device, I show the error message like anyone else, but I do it nicely: I show it in a prominent location on the page, but in a modeless fashion so users can deal with it when they want, not when I want.

There is usually no compelling reason to prevent a user from interacting with other parts of an interface while displaying an error message. That is, nothing about the error is so important that the application thinks, *You absolutely must handle this right now or I'll just die!* There's certainly no reason to stop a user from interacting with the *browser* until he's been notified of the error. That's just . . . crazy.

Instead of relying on rude, implementation-model error notifications, we can be polite. We can go modeless and show users something that lets them continue working, and incidentally maintain their self-esteem. The inline-expand pattern lets us do just that.

▶ Create Forgiving Software

At a deeper level than the need to prevent and detect errors is the need to create software that is forgiving to users as errors occur. Applications should allow users to play around and see what they can do without serious consequences.

A site-builder tool I used recently featured the ability to create forms, such as contact or reservation forms, for a Web site. It wasn't easy to do this, however; it took several minutes just to figure out how to create a new form, add the appropriate form elements (such as text fields and check boxes with labels), and set properties for them (such as their default values and whether or not the fields were required).

After a while of muddling through this grueling process, I attempted to select a text field and delete it. Instead of deleting the single form element, the entire form was removed from the screen. My hard work disappeared forever.

I would have stopped using the application immediately and never looked back, but it was my job at the moment to do an expert review of the application to tell the people who built it how I thought it could be improved. You can probably guess what I reported as my number one recommendation.

An application should never allow users to mess things up so badly that they lose lots of work. Not without some sort of warning. And if a warning cannot be provided in an appealing, non-modal fashion, an undo feature should be provided so that users can quickly backtrack and get moving again.

This bit from Apple's Human Interface Guidelines really says it all:

> *Encourage people to explore your application by building in forgiveness—that is, making most actions easily reversible. People need to feel that they can try things without damaging the system or jeopardizing their data. Create safety nets, such as the Undo and Revert to Saved commands, so that people will feel comfortable learning and using your product.*

Writeboard, another application from 37signals, enables groups of people to collaboratively contribute to a single piece of copy (such as that for the About Us page of a Web site, or a research paper). This application has a rather unique way of allowing users to undo the most serious thing they can do to a Writeboard page: delete it. When a Writeboard is deleted, the user is shown a message indicating an email has been sent to the Writeboard creator that contains a link to recover the page. The link continues to work for seven days. If a user deletes a Writeboard accidentally, he can simply check his email, click the link provided, and be back in good shape in just a few seconds. Or seven days.

You have deleted this writeboard:

"No serious consequences"

An email has been sent to robert@rhjr.net with a link to recover this writeboard. The recovery link will only work for 7 days, after which the writeboard will be permanently deleted.

I have seven whole days to recover my Writeboard once it's deleted.

Writeboard also offers version tracking and comparison. Each time a Writeboard is edited, it can be saved as a new version.

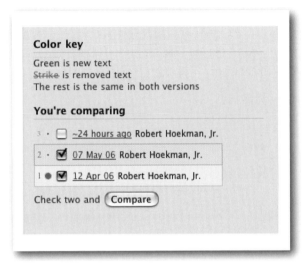

Writeboard's version tracking makes it easy for users to see
what has been done.

Users can at any time compare two versions of the same document by checkmarking the two versions they'd like to see from the list in the sidebar and clicking the **Compare** button (which, incidentally, remains disabled until two document versions are checkmarked—another nice example of a poka-yoke device).

Good software promotes good practices

This topic is a bit fuzzy. It's quite subjective and can only be dealt with on a case-by-case basis, so it requires regular reexamination as we develop new applications.

Promoting good practices, in a nutshell, means that our applications need to make it difficult to produce bad work, and easy to produce good work.

Remember the Web-based site-creation tool? Aside from the disappearing form issue, I found it quite taxing to do anything really well with that tool. The simple act of creating navigation took many steps and involved at least one pop-up window. It was difficult to format text and links, and the end result was a navigation bar that looked almost nothing like I intended. Continuing,

I replaced the default background image for the page's title area with my own, and somehow ended up with two copies of my image, one on top of the other. After a while, I figured out how to get rid of the second one, but the title text itself didn't look quite right. So I accessed the pop-up window required to format text and was very surprised to find none of the text tools applied to the title text. (It turns out the title text wasn't text at all. It was an image, which is why I couldn't edit it. It *looked* like text. How was I to know?) Ultimately, I left the title text the way it was and gave up.

The whole experience was pretty frustrating and left me with a Web page I didn't like that took a lot of time to create. For all the work I had done, I wasn't at all satisfied with the results.

I blamed myself for this, as most users do. I assumed I just didn't get it. I didn't understand some crucial piece of information that would make the whole process make sense. I had missed the basic workflow out of sheer stupidity, and thereby created a page I wouldn't show to my dog.

I realized I was blaming myself and stopped, because how could I, an experienced Web designer, have messed this up so badly if it hadn't been for poor interaction design and weak task flow? And if *I* was messing things up, how much harder was this application to use for people without Web design experience?

This tool made it really easy to produce bad work. I don't ever want to use it again.

Here's the flip side:

Google Page Creator, as previously described, has quite a few good defaults in place. First, it offers a default page template for the user. Second, it offers a default page layout. And when the user enters text into a page she's creating, it relies on default font sizes and colors for body text, headings, and subheadings. This is all very nice and groovy of Google, because it helps users get moving right out of the gate so they can become intermediate users as quickly as possible. But the real key to success for users is that the defaults offered by Google Page Creator promote good practices.

The default template contains an area at the top of the page for a page title, another area in the center for the main content of the page, a space at the bottom for footer information such as a contact link and a copyright disclaimer, and usually some sort of sidebar to be used for persistent navigation. These are all elements typically found in a well-designed Web page.

The default template is also void of annoying tiled background images. It doesn't contain superfluous animations, ad banners, blinking text, or anything else that is known to annoy users.

The default font styles are appropriate for the template as well. A page with a dark background uses a light-colored font. Body text is a standard size and font (10-point Arial). Headings are noticeably larger so visual hierarchy is established. The fonts used for headings and body text complement each other so they look good on the same page.

All of these settings can be changed by the user, but Google Page Creator, by default, guides her toward a page that looks good and adheres to typical design standards for the Web. Since most users stick to the default settings in Web applications, Google Page Creator makes it likely that the user will create a decent page every time. It increases the chances users will produce good work. Users, again, will probably never notice this fact and will attribute success to their own common sense and design savvy. But once again, this is *exactly* the right thing to do. Google doesn't need the credit. Google only needs users to really like Google applications so that they keep coming back to use them.

And users *will* keep coming back. They'll feel so confident after creating a good Web page in just a few minutes that they'll revisit the application to create new pages, to share baby photos and wedding portraits with their families, news from the road while on vacation, and anything else they can think of creating. When Web pages are this easy to build, they'll wonder why all the geeks out there get so wrapped up in programming languages when all you need is Google Page Creator!

It pays to create applications that help users do good work themselves. If your application is meant to help users produce things that will be seen by other people, follow Google's lead and help *your* users look good to *their* users. If you can meet this goal, your users will love your application and will keep coming back.

7

Design for Uniformity, Consistency, and Meaning

▶ Design for Uniformity

▶ Be Consistent Across Applications

▶ Leverage Irregularity to Create Meaning and Importance

Design is the difference between this and a form that is easy to analyze and understand.

Nature.com's article "Web users judge sites in the blink of an eye" reports that users can make judgments about a Web site in just 50 milliseconds.

The article states:

> We all know that first impressions count, but this study shows that the brain can make flash judgments almost as fast as the eye can take in the information. The discovery came as a surprise to some experts. 'My colleagues believed it would be impossible to really see anything in less than 500 milliseconds,' says Gitte Lindgaard of Carleton University in Ottawa, who has published the research in the journal Behaviour and Information Technology. Instead they found that impressions were made in the first 50 milliseconds of viewing.
>
> Lindgaard and her team presented volunteers with the briefest glimpses of Web pages previously rated as being either easy on the eye or particularly jarring, and asked them to rate the websites on a sliding scale of visual appeal. Even though the images flashed up for just 50 milliseconds, roughly the duration of a single frame of standard television footage, their verdicts tallied well with judgments made after a longer period of scrutiny.

Pay close attention to that last sentence. It says, basically, that users maintain similar impressions about the visual appeal of a site in the long term to those made within the first 50 milliseconds. The first impression is solid and incredibly important.

Does this mean that users actually judge a site this quickly? Do the first 50 milliseconds make so much of an impression that users actually decide if the site is appealing?

In a word: yes.

The first 50 milliseconds is not enough time to determine whether the information on a site is useful, where on the landing page to find information, or learn anything about the site. It's a super-fast first impression.

All I could absorb in a 50-millisecond test was the background color, the fact that there was an image on the page, and that content appeared to be laid out in columns. I couldn't discern the subject of the photo, the content of the columns, the company name or logo, or anything meaningful. This hyper-speed glance did not show me whether the site was going to be meaningful for me or not, but it *did* give me enough time to know it wasn't one of those obnoxious, brightly-colored sites generated by Microsoft Word about someone's cat. This is useful information, since it's highly unlikely I'll ever need information from such a site, so it turns out that 50 milliseconds was indeed enough to tell me the site might contain something useful and was at least well-designed enough that I might be able to find what I needed.

At 500 milliseconds, elements were much more discernable. I had enough time to recognize that the photo was of a woman with a baby, there were three columns on the page, there was a text field on the left (probably a Search box), and that there were some icons on the right. It was still not enough for me to decide if I was going to leave the site or stay and try to find the information I needed, but it was definitely enough to ascertain I was staring at a well-designed site that I could probably trust to contain valuable information.

Uniformity, visual hierarchy, structure, flow, meaning, and consistency are vital tools in the job of making a great first impression, because these things allow a user to analyze pages quickly and make sense of them. Consistent and uniform design also allows users to rely on what's known as "spatial memory" (more on this later in this chapter).

All these things contribute to a simple, obvious design. One that helps users form a mental model which enables them to be productive without having to think about how an application works.

For example, users shouldn't need to determine (even subconsciously) whether one large object on a page is more important than another. Even tiny inconsistencies cause small blips in the brain that are enough to throw off a user's workflow and interrupt an otherwise calm and productive state of mind. Any time we can maintain consistency to eliminate these interruptions, we give the user another reason to trust our applications, and we create a way to leverage *irregularities* to create meaning and importance (more on this later on this chapter).

The ability to design these qualities is both the result of everything talked about in this book so far and a necessary ingredient for an obvious design.

(You can read Nature.com's article at **www.nature.com/news/2006/060109/ full/060109-13.html**, but unfortunately, you must be a Premium Plus subscriber to access the information.)

▶ Design for Uniformity

When a builder puts together a staircase, uniformity is about making sure each step is the same height and depth so that people don't trip all over themselves while heading up or down. (Can you imagine a staircase where one step is 4" high and 6" deep, the next 12" high and 3" deep, and so on? You'd have to examine every step to decide how to proceed.)

When designing interfaces, things are not all that different. Elements such as visual hierarchy, proportion, alignment, and typography play major parts in the uniformity of a design, and each must be designed so that users can quickly extract meaning from each screen and form a mental model with which to work.

Visual hierarchy

When markup code is written properly, titles are titles and paragraphs are paragraphs. Semantic code is written so that content is organized like a term paper, with headings, subheadings, body text, and so on. When this is done, pages are more organized by default, because HTML renders headings larger than other elements, each heading type defaults to gradually descending font sizes, and body text is shown smallest so it's clearly separated from the headings.

All this adds up to a page that can be analyzed at a glance, because the user can immediately see what's most important on a page and what on the page lends support to the first element. This allows him to make a snap judgment about whether to stay because the page contains useful information, or to leave because it does not. It also allows him to quickly find a link that might lead him to other useful information.

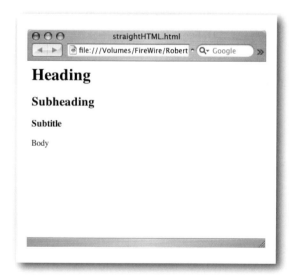

HTML organizes content into a visual hierarchy on its own. No wheel-reinventing needed.

When creating the user interface for a Web application with semantic code, these elements can be created easily and maintained across multiple screens to provide a sort of built-in meaning for users. Users can quickly recognize the relationships between headings and content because each has its own default display settings that make the organization clear.

Sticking to the basics and letting HTML do what it does best—define structure for written content—is a clean and simple way to ensure visual hierarchy. Yes, page elements should be styled to create the look and feel you want for your application, but the CSS used to style the elements should support what HTML is designed to do on its own. Headings should be big and obvious and body text should be small while remaining clearly legible. Supporting the natural tendencies of HTML keeps things clear.

Proportion

Proportion is defined by the size or quantity of certain elements as compared to others.

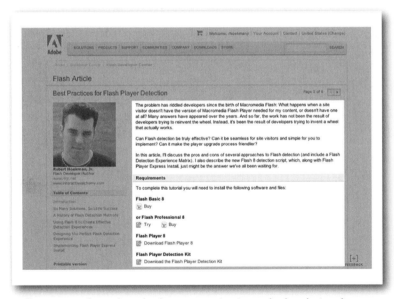

Sadly, content often takes a back seat to navigation and other design elements.

The average Web page (and the homepage in particular) uses only about 20–30 percent of its available space for actual content. The rest is made up of header graphics, navigational elements, footer content, ad banners, white space, and images that don't directly support the content. In Web applications, this figure may vary wildly depending on the design, but most of what appears on a given application screen is there to orient users to the site itself, not the content.

Designers tend to focus their page designs around making sure the user knows where he is on the site, what site he is using, how he can get to other sections, and so on. (Of course, they do this because countless usability studies have told us it's a good idea, so they're right to do so.) And graphical elements meant to give an application its look and feel (referred to by many designers as the "chrome") often take up as much as 1/3 of the visible space on a screen. Add a little white space and advertising to that, along with even the simplest of navigational elements, and it's a wonder we have any room left at all. This proportion of pixels to data means Web applications often suffer from long, scrolling pages and a lack of **findability** (the ability to find a particular element easily).

However, the content is the most important part of the application. Minimizing chrome to leave plenty of room for the interaction elements is crucial to helping users be productive. Just as much as error and confirmation messages get in a user's way, excess chrome can be a big annoyance when trying to move around within an application. Having a large proportion of non-essential elements is a sure way to detract from those things that are most important in a screen.

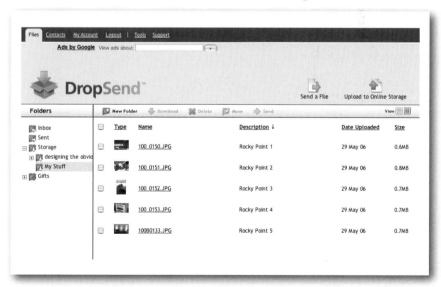

Ahhh . . . room to breathe.

DropSend is a nice example of how to minimize chrome and leave plenty of breathing room for data display. The principal purpose of this application is to manage files, and chrome would just get in the way. So Carson Systems decided to focus the interface on the content instead of the tool. The graphical elements that make up the interface have been minimized to allow a wide-open view of the files a user has uploaded. Even within this layout, there is room to minimize chrome further by tightening up the space used for the header. The logo could be a bit smaller and the main divider bar could be shifted up the page a bit further. But this interface, when compared to Box.net, is nice and open.

Content in Box.net, again, gets less room than the rest of the interface.

Box wastes a lot of space by packing the entire interface into a small area in the center of the page. Moving the sidebar to the left edge of the page and making the rest of the interface stretch to the right edge would really open up the area used to display the list of uploaded files.

The proportion of the page taken up by graphical elements (or not used at all) is pretty big, and as a result, Box limits its display of actual data to roughly 1/3 of the page (depending on screen resolution and size of the browser window).

DropSend, on the other hand, leaves a good chunk of the available screen real estate open for content. The design allows users to get a better at-a-glance view of the files they are managing, and gets the interface out of the way.

Every screen in DropSend is designed this way. It enables users to work with any new screen as easily as the last, and the simple layout helps users form a simple picture of the purpose of the application and an effective initial mental model. (The only thing I don't like about the DropSend interface, in fact, is the tree view control, which could easily be revised to simplify the navigation of directory levels, as shown in Chapter 4.)

Alignment

Many of us played the classic "one of these things is not like the other" games when we were children, designed to further enhance our innate ability to discern one thing from another. We'd stare at pictures containing three rubber ducks and a fire hydrant and scream with delight, "*That* one is not the same!" We prided ourselves on our ability to pick out the thing that didn't match.

As we age, these lessons stay with us (in addition to our intrinsic, human ability to notice difference). When we see something that doesn't match up, we wonder why, even if only subconsciously. When fields in a registration form all line up to the left edge except for one field that's 12 pixels to the right, we think about it. Does it mean something? Why is this one out of place? We're hard-wired to see the *differences*.

Alignment is about avoiding difference. Newspapers, books, Word documents, floor plans, and millions of other things are designed so that various elements are aligned to each other: Groups of elements are aligned to one side, others to another side, everything is aligned to a common top edge, and so on. Without uniform alignment, books and sites are much more difficult to read because we have to constantly evaluate whether the positioning is meaningful.

There isn't necessarily anything wrong with a non-aligned design. Sometimes it's used intentionally. But the goal of a Web application is usually to enable a user to get something specific done in an efficient manner, and messiness detracts from this goal. Uniform alignment is key to streamlining the process because it ensures that nothing distracts the user while she is trying to complete the task at hand.

Form elements in Web pages, for example, should be aligned to each other. If the widest text area on the page is 250 pixels wide, then all other elements should line up to the right edge of that text area. They should all be justified to each other's left edge, span the same width, be distributed evenly and consistently from each other (for example, if two fields are 10 pixels apart vertically, all others should be as well), and generally form a large rectangle when the page is looked at in terms of geometrical shapes so that no individual element stands out and makes users think it means something more than the others.

Meebo's registration form is designed uniformly – the fields form a straight line on both the left and right edges.

With everything flowing in a straight line down the page, the page is easy to read at a glance and minimizes the effort required to understand what the page is about and how to deal with it.

Typography

Much like misaligned objects on a screen, users notice differences in fonts, font sizes, colors, and so on, and attribute meaning to them. Consistent typography, like uniform alignment, enables users to stay focused on the task instead of wondering what to infer about each difference in font.

Fortunately, there are a few hard and fast rules that have become standard on the Web when it comes to typography.

First, never use different fonts from screen to screen. Make a decision and stick with it. This is the simplest way to ensure consistency from page to page within an application.

Second, choose one typeface for the big, pop-off-the-page elements like headings, and choose a second typeface for the rest of the content. These two typefaces should differ enough from each other that the difference appears intentional. If the typefaces are too similar, headings and such can blend too easily into the rest of the page, and the meaning otherwise implied by clearly distinct typefaces can be lost.

Third, never use more than two or three different fonts. In fact, three is often too many. Multiple typefaces on a single screen can be disorienting, making it harder for the user to easily find what she is looking for.

Finally, limit the colors and sizes used for fonts. Of course, headings should be larger than body text, and body text should be larger than footer content, but avoid using different font sizes within body text. Also, use as few colors as possible. Choose colors for headings, body text, footers, links, visited links, active links, and so on, and use those choices for every page.

When it comes to typography on the Web, the less you do, the better.

Spatial memory

Spatial memory is the ability to recall where physical objects are in relation to other objects. It's what allows us to move around in a dark, but familiar, room. As we step into the room and fumble for the light switch, we can find it because we remember where it is located on the wall. If we continue into the room without turning on the light, perhaps to grab something off a desk, we can usually safely move around without bumping into objects and potentially

injuring ourselves. Our brains can recall the locations of the desk, the chair, the item on the desk, and other furniture using spatial memory.

Our users navigate pages using spatial memory. After a user has interacted with a page a few times, he forms a subconscious knowledge of the relative locations of elements on the page. He moves his mouse pointer without looking and without thinking. When every page contains the same navigational elements, in the same location as all the others, this is easy to do. Users can reliably jump to the point on the page where they know a button is located and click without having to really think about it.

Spatial memory is made up of three parts. First, a user must know what items are present on a page. Second, he must know where the items are located in relation to other items on the page. Finally, he must know where his mouse pointer currently rests in relation to each item. This is how the user forms a mental map of the page so he can move around without much effort.

It takes very little time for users to form these mental maps. The first couple of times a person uses a site, he learns where the persistent navigation is located and what links are contained within the element. From then on, he can move around the space more easily because spatial memory goes to work and he no longer has to evaluate the page in its entirety every single time to figure it out.

Consistent layout supports this behavior. So does proper alignment, because it's much simpler to move to something that appears in a straight line with everything else than it is to move the mouse to somewhat arbitrary spot in the middle of a bunch of content.

▶ Be Consistent Across Applications

Companies that create Web applications usually put out more than one. And a company that bases its business on the sale of Web applications wants to convey a consistent brand, consistent level of quality, and consistent user experience. When this is the case, it's important to look at all the applications put out by the company to see how they mesh.

Without consistency, a company's brand can end up on shaky ground. When customers are forced to learn a dramatically different interface with each application, the company itself can look as though it lacks focus and a clear purpose. Using different sign-on screens for every application, an inconsistent appearance, different approaches for similar task flows, and distinct design patterns for otherwise identical interactions forces users to work to learn new information all the time. Users don't like that.

Learning to use one application should make learning all the others easier. Not only is this better for users, it's better for us. Consistency allows us to more easily convert customers already happy with one application into customers who will be happy with new ones. Consistency in design allows one success to be built upon another.

Consistency in design also means new applications can be put together in less time and with less energy. Reusing interface paradigms already proven effective in current applications means new solutions will be easier to learn for users, easier to develop, easier to design, and more effective right out of the gate.

Consistent messaging

In addition to everything else you can do to maintain consistency, it's important to make sure system messages remain consistent as well. In fact, it's actually easier to do this than to create different types of message displays for different scenarios. Once a system is in place for the display of messages, it can be reused over and over via a simple function in the code. I highly recommend implementing such a system in each application you create so that messages are always as simple to display as a function call, and users know what is happening every time a message is displayed and never have to wonder why the differences exist.

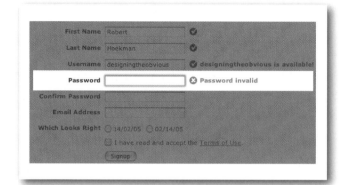

Consistent messaging allows users to trust they know what to expect from an application. No surprises, no thought.

Understanding design patterns

Design patterns are a powerful tool when trying to maintain consistent user experiences across multiple interactions within a single application and across multiple applications (for example, when several applications by the same company are integrated to work together). These patterns are the glue that holds everything together.

Design patterns are used all over the Web because they allow software designers to leverage the experience users have from other sites in their own applications to make them easier to learn.

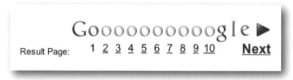

The pagination design used by Google is used by many other search engines as well, so no one has to struggle with understanding a new design.

The design used for pagination in most search engines, for example, looks very similar in almost every case, and is used so widely because it works in such a way that users no longer have to think about how pagination works (or even that it's called "pagination"). Users can simply glance at the series of numbered links, wrapped with **Previous** and **Next** links, and know what to do.

For more information on design patterns, I highly recommend checking out Jennifer Tidwell's book *Designing Interfaces* (O'Reilly). It's a tremendous resource on the subject, and anyone designing Web applications for a living would be wise to read every page. It's the kind of book that should take up permanent residence on an application designer's bookshelf, much like Strunk and White's *The Elements of Style* is kept on a writer's bookshelf. That said, you can check out most of the design patterns themselves via the book's support site, **www.designinginterfaces.com**.

While you're online reading up on patterns, consider checking out the blog discussion on the subject over at **www.lukew.com**. Luke Wroblewski is the principal designer at Yahoo, Inc. and the author of *Site-Seeing: A Visual Approach to Web Usability*. In May of 2006, he used his blog to conduct a discussion between himself and several other designers (including Jennifer Tidwell and James Reffel, the UI design manager for eBay) about the power of design patterns and what they mean. The first in the series of posts can be found at **www.lukew.com/ff/entry.asp?347**.

Design pattern libraries

Possibly the greatest thing a designer can do to help ensure consistency across applications (and even throughout a single application) is to create a design pattern library.

As previously described, design patterns are the glue that holds everything together in an interface. They help users learn new applications based on experience with others (e.g., the pagination element used at the bottom of many search results pages) and can be used across multiple applications to support a consistent user experience.

A **design pattern library** is a collection of design patterns that have been documented so designers and developers can reuse the paradigms that have been proven to work and that maintain consistency across applications.

A pattern library can come in the form of a wiki for multi-user collaboration or even a simple PowerPoint document with just a few slides. The important thing is that each pattern has a name, a description of when and how to use it, and preferably a screenshot or wireframe of a possible implementation of the pattern so others can easily put the descriptions into context.

Jennifer Tidwell's www.designinginterfaces.com site is a pattern library, but one that serves a broad range of applications instead of a focused set of solutions provided by a single company. The patterns found there can be abstracted and used in any company's internal library, or can simply be used as a reference encyclopedia whenever you get stuck on a design problem.

In the case of a company-specific library, the patterns usually pertain to the solutions the company has devised for their own applications. If all of the company's tools, for example, are meant to use the same basic layout and pagination structure, its design pattern library contains patterns that explain the details.

Patterns can be as broad as a general framework for a design solution or as specific as describing exact details about how each solution should work (e.g., "If more than five options are to be presented, a dropdown menu should be used instead of radio buttons, and the menu should be set to an appropriate default value."). Whatever the case, a pattern library is a great tool for a company to have in its toolbox. Disparate teams building applications for the same company can rely on the library to determine how to handle almost any design problem and still end up with a solution consistent with the company's other tools. This benefits the company, its users, and the internal design staff, who can spend less time answering questions about how interfaces should work and more time evolving the company's products to support a long-term vision.

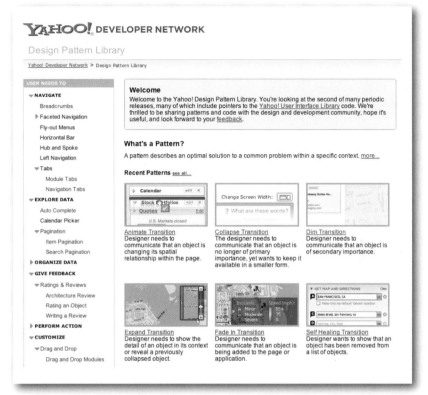

The Yahoo! Design Pattern Library is one of the best resources on the Web for a glimpse into how pattern libraries should be created.

To see another example of a design pattern library, swing by developer.yahoo. com/ypatterns, where Yahoo! shares its own patterns with the public. This library features patterns as generalized as grid-based page layouts and as specific as the Drag and Drop Modules pattern used by My Yahoo!, Google Personalized, and even Dashboard HQ to handle the reorganization of content modules on a customizable page.

Yahoo! also offers a code base that can be used to implement many of the patterns in Web applications. It's available through the Yahoo! User Interface Library at developer.yahoo.com/yui.

Intelligent inconsistency

Well-known user experience designer Mark Hurst mentioned "intelligent incon-sistency" in a blog post titled "The Page Paradigm" (www.goodexperience.com/blog/archives/000028.php). In the context of that post, intelligent inconsistency is about providing only what's necessary on a given Web page even if it results in inconsistencies in navigation and other design elements. This is potentially dangerous advice, because many newer designers won't always have the ability to make truly wise decisions about when and how to be inconsistent, but the concept has merit with regard to interface design in general.

Sometimes it's better to be inconsistent than to maintain consistency at all costs. For example, a purchase path (the sequence of screens shown to a user when she is making a purchase on a site) might show different add-on offers based on what the user is purchasing. In this case, it makes more sense to show appropriate add-on offers than to offer the same ones regardless of the user's interests (intelligent add-ons are much more profitable). Likewise, it makes sense to show a Cancel button only when canceling is a likely and necessary choice, whereas most interactions don't really need this option. (In most cases, a Cancel option is just plain unnecessary, despite the fact that it's provided in the vast majority of online forms.)

Knowing when to be inconsistent is the mark of experience. If you don't feel comfortable enough yet with your ability to decide when and where to be inconsistent, err on the side of consistency.

▶ Leverage Irregularity to Create Meaning and Importance

This is the part where I pull a bait-and-switch on you. After all this talk about consistent design and uniformity, telling you to leverage irregularity may seem a little insane. But this concept comes straight from the basics of design knowledge, and is vital to the representation of data and interface elements in an application.

Uniform and consistent design, as we've discussed, is key to helping users extract meaning from the design of an application and keeping them focused on tasks. But sometimes we need to make something stand out a bit on purpose so users realize it actually *is* more important than other elements, or at least different somehow, and requires additional attention. When this happens, we need to stray from the rules of uniformity.

The best way to make something stand out is to present it differently than everything else. Much like the notion of creating applications that stand out by taking a completely new approach to the completion of a common activity, irregularity is a great way to make individual elements on a single page stand out from others. And the same tools used to design uniformity and consistency can be used to make page elements unique. In fact, consistent and uniform interfaces make it *possible* for things to stand out. Uniqueness is the product of *difference*, and difference can only occur in an environment of sameness.

Rollyo uses color and dimension to make its Search box stand out from other page elements.

For example, Rollyo features a Search box on its homepage (and every other page, for that matter) because the primary purpose of the site is to allow users to search content. To make the Search box stand out, Rollyo increased the dimensions of the text field, wrapped it in a nice, colorful Rollyo logo graphic, and set the font to a much larger size than other content on a Rollyo page. The Search box is easy to spot on every page and, as a bonus, reinforces the Rollyo brand every time it appears.

Google's Search box, also readily available throughout the application, is set apart by always being displayed next to the Google logo.

Making something stand out is not complicated. It's usually a simple matter of *making it stand out*. (I love it when things are obvious.)

That said, there is one small thing to keep in mind. If something is meant to stand out, the element should be inconsistent enough from the rest of the interface that it appears to have been done intentionally. Small differences in alignment, coloring, and dimension may appear accidental and decrease a user's confidence. Big differences, on the other hand, make it clear that whatever was done was intentional.

Color

Color is a great way to make something stand out. It's also the simplest. When everything in an interface is blue and white, for example, a red error message sticks out like a sore thumb.

When deciding which colors to use throughout an application, reserve one or two additional colors for things that need to stand out from everything else. Just make sure the contrasting colors play well with the color palette you choose for the rest of the site. Making something stand out shouldn't mean completely disrupting your design.

Simple as that.

Since the predominant page color here is light blue, the Yahoo! Search box, which uses a slightly darker shade of blue, draws the eye right to it.

Color differences can also be very subtle. If the predominant color of a page is light blue, a page element using a slightly darker shade of blue easily distinguishes itself from the rest of the page. Subtle differences like this can be just enough to draw the user's eye to the element without being disruptive to the flow of the page. Sharper differences, however, are more effective when a page element is particularly important and *must* be noticed. In this case, use strong, contrasting colors.

Dimension

As I mentioned earlier in this book, Odeo.com has a gigantic registration form. Nothing else on the site is nearly as large. I'm not sure why. The size of the form fields is distracting and not at all necessary. It appears to have been made large just to avoid what could otherwise be a barren page. The registration screen has only four fields, but it takes up a good chunk of screen real estate. There's nothing else on the registration screen, so it's unnecessary to use increased dimensions to imply importance. With no other visible content, the importance is implied by default.

That said, elements that take up a lot of room are viewed as more important, mainly *because* they take up more room and smaller elements convey lesser importance. Dimension can define what's most important on each page by simply making an individual element stand out from the others by its size.

If you use dimension to make a page element stand out from the others, be sure to make the proportional increase in dimension consistent from page to page as well. The consistency will, again, help a user reliably know that a large element equates to an important one as she moves around the application.

If elements are sized differently each time, she may find herself wondering why, and the whole goal is to avoid this.

Interface Surgery: Surfacing the bananas in a process

Seth Godin posits in *The Big Red Fez* that users follow trails of clear, distinct signposts much in the same way that monkeys follow trails of bananas. In other words, if you add a button to a page that tells users exactly what you want them to do, and it meshes with what they want to do, they'll click it. It's a strange metaphor, but it does do a great job of illustrating yet another way to design the obvious. And designing page elements to stand out is exactly how we can achieve this effect.

I can't tell you whether or not Ryan Carson ever read *The Big Red Fez*, but he does seem to have gotten the point. He says:

> *We had to keep reminding ourselves that DropSend is meant to solve one problem, and one problem only: sending large files that you can't email.*
>
> *We were constantly tempted to introduce new features, but we always said no. Thankfully, we have received many compliments on how easy it is to use DropSend, so I guess we achieved that aim.*

(Of course, DropSend can be used for *any* file you want to store online, not just large files, but the application was designed specifically to support files too large to send by email.)

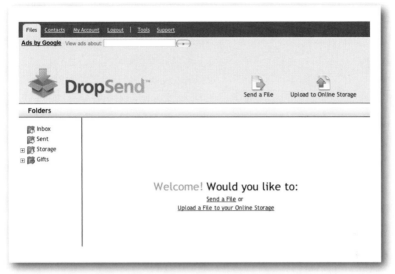

DropSend features a banana to help you get started.

Upon logging into DropSend, the basic interface shell is displayed, but in the center of the main content area is a very obvious block of text that asks if you want to <u>Send a File</u> or <u>Upload a File to Your Online Storage</u>.

This is a banana. It tells the user how to get started. It tells her what Carson Systems hopes she will do while she's logged into DropSend. It also tells her how to do what *she* wants to do.

Bananas are incredibly useful when you want the user to do something specific, like complete a task. For example, a user wishing to purchase a new desk chair needs to locate the chair she wants, add it to her shopping cart, enter her billing information, and confirm the purchase. This process is much easier to follow when each screen in the process uses a banana to guide her towards completion of the task.

Surfacing the bananas in a Web page is a matter of understanding what is most important on the page and then making it stand out somehow. Sometimes there may be more than one important element on a page, but in most cases, there should not be more than three or four. If there are more bananas than this, odds are the design is not as focused as it should be, and users are being given too many options.

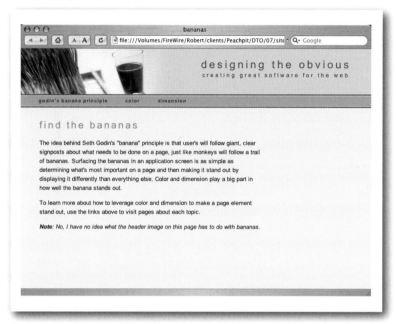

No bananas here.

Pages containing a lot of text do not always do a great job of surfacing the bananas in a process. The intent of the screen shown here is to compel the user to learn about Godin's banana principle by reading the three pages that explain the concept and how to achieve it. But ironically, although the text explains how to do this, there is no clear and obvious path towards the completion of the task. Sure, there is a navigation element towards the top of the screen, but the goal is to get the user moving quickly and in the right direction.

The first thing we can do is convert the terms within the text that point to the appropriate pages into links.

This minor change can certainly help anyone who bothers to read the text on this page, but odds are, not many people will stick around long enough to find the links. We need to put up some big signs that explain what to do.

Links are easy to spot within large blocks of text, but this page still lacks a banana.

Bananas for everyone!

In this version, the graphical buttons indicate the actions the user should take. The new design points the user to the three pages and offers an obvious way to access each one. It also takes focus off the text.

These buttons use the same colors as the rest of the page, but since the main content area does not contain the dark green and red colors, the buttons stand out. They also stand out by appearing larger than everything else on the page. The buttons use a larger font than even the page title and logo areas of the page.

The final version of the page leverages color and dimension to make the bananas stand out.

And since the buttons now tell the user exactly what to do, we can remove the text telling the user to "use the links above to visit pages about each topic." The new, shortened version makes the block of text look even less important when compared to the buttons.

Godin's banana principle doesn't apply to everything. Portal pages and the like are not good candidates for large, clear signposts, because they are generally aimed at offering users a wide variety of options instead of just a couple. But when the mission for the company and the user is to move the user through a particular set of screens towards completion of a goal, bananas can be very effective.

Consistency and uniformity help users understand applications, derive meaning from screens, and stay on track without a lot of effort. But when it's particularly important for the user to focus on a certain page element, changes in color and dimension can be just the thing to make it pop off the page and communicate to the user what needs to be done.

8

Reduce and Refine

- ▶ Clean Up the Mess
- ▶ Practice Kaizen
- ▶ Eliminate Waste
- ▶ Put Just-In-Time Design and Review To Work

Every element on a page fights for the attention of the user. Text sits next to form elements, which sit next to ad banners, which sit next to logos, taglines, copyright information, and persistent navigation. How is a user supposed to know which things *really* need attention and which things can safely be ignored?

Interfaces full of unnecessary graphical elements, text that's longer than it needs to be, and features that don't really help anyone risk creating an environment of visual overload. Every time a user accesses a page, his brain must take a moment to process everything on the screen to see what's there and analyze the importance of each element. This moment can be disorienting when a page is jammed full of content and graphics.

Clutter diminishes a user's ability to form a workable mental model by crowding the important pieces of a screen in with unimportant ones. Clutter makes it more difficult for new users to become intermediate users by putting things in the way of the learning process. Clutter makes it hard to see the *design* in the design.

Clutter makes a mess of things.

Cluttered interfaces result in comments like:

"It's as though the marketing department threw up on this page."

Ouch.

Cluttered task flows

But clutter doesn't apply only to individual screens. It also applies to interactions and task flows.

The task-management system I use, for example, displays the Task Detail page every time I finish editing a task. This fact, in and of itself, is fine, and it makes sense. I do usually want to see the final version of the task details once I've completed editing the page. But there's no ability to add a new task to the project I'm currently working with from the Task Detail screen, so I have to click a rather insignificant text link, displayed amongst loads of other text, to return to the Project screen and then click again to create a new task. This would be no big deal if I only used the application once a week, and only edited or added a couple of tasks at a time, but I often need to set up a new project and define a series of tasks all at once.

Every time I finish creating one task, I have to click back over to the Project screen to add the next new task. Since projects generally involve many individual tasks, I have to do this upwards of 10 or 15 times within a half hour. One little link on the Task Details screen (something like **Create New Task**) would cure this completely. Without the link, the process of setting up a new project involves reloading the Project page over and over again when I have no need to view the Project screen in the first place. This clutters up the workflow unnecessarily, because it means I have to constantly revisit screens I *don't* want to see to get to the ones I *do* want to see.

Drives me nuts.

The path to simplicity

It's not always possible to keep a Web-based application simple. There are some incredibly complicated applications out there, for good reason. Despite this, designing the obvious means striving for simplicity.

In the book *Designing Visual Interfaces*, authors Mullet and Sano state:

> *Reduction through successive refinement is the only path to simplicity.*

Every word in this sentence speaks volumes. "Reduction" tells us to reduce the scope of our software, stripping it down to what's really needed. "Successive refinement" tells us to iterate; don't stop at a single design and call it a day. Keep iterating, re-evaluating, challenging yourself to make the design cleaner, simpler, and more elegant (and thusly, more purposeful). And "simplicity" clearly references the principle goal of application design.

Making a complicated application clear requires making each piece of it as simple as possible. Designing the obvious means reducing and refining each screen, each task flow, and each interaction so that the purpose and function is as simple as possible.

When each piece of an application is reduced to its simplest form, the application as a whole achieves clarity.

DropSend limits the number of graphical elements used so as to maximize the space allowed for the display of stored files. Backpack leverages inline editing features to reduce the complexity of tasks so users avoid round-trip interactions where editing is done on administrative pages. JotSpot Live includes only the bare essential graphic elements on a given page to lessen the visual load of each page and focus completely on the ability to create and review notes. Google Page Creator reduces the number of features, including only the 20 percent needed by most people to create an effective and simple Web page quickly. Box.net lets you upload multiple files at once to reduce the time it takes to do the task.

All of these applications have a narrow scope, include only what's absolutely essential, rely on clean and simple interfaces, feature screens that are light on text, and focus entirely on the task at hand.

All of these qualities contribute to a simplified user experience and help reduce the complexity of their respective applications by avoiding clutter, both mental and physical.

▶ Clean Up the Mess

For people to use our software, they need to be able to find the features they need. We need to unbury the things that make our applications great and put a giant spotlight on them. The best way to do this is to reduce clutter in the screens that comprise our application interfaces.

As discussed in Chapter 7, contrast (often created through color and dimension) is an effective tool for making a particular part of a screen stand out. This is true because some things are *seen* before a user even begins paying real attention to particular elements. A bright red box on a page comprised of only shades of blue, for example, is seen first because it sharply contrasts with everything else on the screen. Before our brains ever register what's going on, we see the red box. But although contrast is one of the most effective ways to make something stand out from the crowd, it's not the only solution.

Another rather obvious way to ensure that an interface element is seen is to remove anything that takes a user's attention *away* from it.

Reducing the pixel-to-data ratio

The very same artwork that provides the look and feel for an application is also one of the biggest culprits of clutter in interfaces. The space that graphics take up, the colors used, the proportion of graphics to information, and the overall tone of graphical elements can all detract from the content of an application and take focus away from what matters. Reducing the volume of graphical elements is one of the best ways to eliminate clutter.

Usable, yes. Personable, no.

This is not to say we should all design our applications to emulate the *un-design* of Jakob Nielsen's Web site at www.useit.com. Nielsen may be a major guru of Web usability, but it's more than possible to design an application that is both clean and aesthetically appealing.

Logos, for example, don't need to take up a lot of room, but they often do. Product names, product logos, and corporate logos are often displayed at rather large sizes near the top of application screens, despite being probably the least important elements on a page.

I understand the urge to spotlight these elements. Marketing departments want to create brand recognition. It's a reasonable request. What they often forget is that by the time the user sees the giant product name and company logo, she's already decided to use the product. Using screen real estate to repeatedly tell her the name of the product is only going to limit how much space can be used for more important content.

The best marketing tool you can have is a well-designed application.

Users appreciate your well-designed application far more than they appreciate having the company name shoved in their faces every time they load a new screen. Feel free to add a logo to the application, but keep it small and bury it in a corner of the page so it's out of the way. Don't focus on logos. Focus on benefits.

Also, try to keep layers of organizational graphics to a minimum. Far too often, Web applications organize individual sections into boxes and end up with so many levels of nested boxes that the simple divider-line graphics used to make such divisions take up dozens of pixels for no reason at all.

If sections of the design can be segregated without the use of boxes, do it. If page elements can be grouped into fewer individual areas and take up less space, do that, too. Whatever can be done to reduce the space used and the ratio of pixels to data will help the application's functionality and benefits shine through.

Minimizing copy

A lot has been said about minimizing copy online. (Isn't irony fun?) But some of the wisest words have shown up in, of all places, books.

Strunk and White's *The Elements of Style*, for example, is always a great source for learning to write more concisely and vigorously, and the standards defined by this book apply every bit as much to the Web as they do to print.

One of the guidelines offered in the book is "Omit needless words." Steve Krug had a little fun with this axiom in his own book, *Don't Make Me Think*, by titling a chapter "Omit needless words" and crossing out the word "needless."

Removing words is a sure-fire way to reduce clutter in an interface, but it can be difficult to decide what to cut and how to revise what's left. Here are some guidelines:

- **Move instructive copy into <u>What's This?</u> Help documentation.** Much of the text that clutters up interfaces is instructive. Developers often assume that users will thoroughly read the instructions. They don't.

   Users typically skip right over anything textual and go straight to guessing. They click the first thing that looks like it might help them do what they need to do. So instead of cluttering up an interface with instructions, convert them to inline Help documents. Replace the text in the application screen with a <u>What's This?</u> link that either opens a popup window that contains the text or displays the text inline using the inline-expand design pattern discussed in Chapter 6.

- **Write vigorously.** In a Web application, you have very little chance of grabbing a user's attention with text (applications are about *doing*, not reading). So when text absolutely must be included, keep it concise. Omit needless words, limit the text to its core message, and try to break up paragraphs into shorter, more succinct bullet lists using as few words as possible.

- **Avoid happy talk.** "Happy talk" is what Steve Krug calls the text on a Web page that aims only to tell the user how great the company or the application is, without backing it up with any real substance. It doesn't tell the user what to do, how to get started, how to complete a task, or even how an application might benefit the user. Instead, it uses buzzwords and self-congratulatory statements like "We were the first development team to land on the moon while simultaneously eating breakfast, standing on one foot, and patting our heads."

   Happy talk is most likely to be found on the introductory, pre-registration screens for an application, such as the home page (you know, the page that's supposed to be one of the most important marketing tools you have).

Get rid of the happy talk. Show screenshots, a giant **Try It Now** button, a tagline that summarizes the application's purpose, and a link to a (well-compressed) video about how the application works and what it does.

- **Use trigger words instead of a lot of words.** A modicum of trigger words is better than a lot of really informative words. Informative text is informative only if anyone reads it. And no one will. If you must include text in your interface, be sure that text includes words the user might actually look for (according to *their* mental model and experience level, not yours) or that will jump out and grab the user's attention. And if the text is *really* important, refer back to Chapter 7 to see how to make it stand out.

Designing white space

Wichita State University's Software Usability Research Laboratory (SURL) posted an article in October 2003 about the merits of **white space** and how it affects the usability and aesthetic appeal of a Web page. White space is any area that appears blank on a screen. It describes the buffer of empty pixels provided between areas of a page to separate them, as well as the surrounding empty spaces provided to create page margins.

SURL performed usability tests to assess the differences in performance and visual appeal of varying amounts of white space in response to a 1997 report from Web usability researcher Jared Spool that sites using more white space are inferior to more dense sites, with regard to a user's ability to find information. Three versions of the same Web page were created using varying amounts of white space (low, medium, and high amounts). Each version of the page was shown to five of 15 testers, so each person saw only one version.

What SURL discovered in their own tests is that there was no significant difference in the time it took for users to find information relevant to the proposed tasks (such as, "A friend of yours is interested in hiking the backwoods of Alaska or the jungles of the Amazon basin of South America. Find the site that mentions both of these areas."), but there were differences in the aesthetic appeal of the three different versions of the page.

Users were more satisfied with the version of the page that used a medium level of white space. They felt that a high amount of white space made the page slower because it required more scrolling to access content, but also felt that too dense of a layout made the page less readable than the others.

The tests, basically, were the white space equivalent of the story of Goldilocks and the Three Bears (without the part where the user runs out of the lab, never to be seen again). One version of the page had too much white space, while another had too little. The third, however, was "just right."

So, while white space had no apparent effect on a user's ability to complete a task, it had a great effect on how much the user *enjoyed* the page.

This, as you can see, makes the act of designing white space a bit dicey, because "medium" is a relative term, so a designer's ability to allow a medium amount of white space is contingent on his own definition of the term and his analysis of individual screens.

Incidentally, the part of the report that indicates that the amount of white space had no effect on the time it took for users to find information should probably be ignored. The tasks users were asked to perform during SURL's usability tests all involved searching for an appropriate link within the page, which contained nothing but three columns of black text on a white background, and section headings and a page title displayed in dark red text. Links appeared as default HTML hyperlinks, which means they displayed as underlined blue text.

Blue links stick out like a sore thumb on a page that contains nothing but text on a white background.

As you know from reading Chapter 7, color is one of the best ways to make something stand out on a page, and underlined blue text links stand out extremely well on a page full of black text. A user asked to look for a link on a Web page like this needs only to glance at the page, regardless of how much white space is used, to quickly spot all the instances of underlined blue text. Because the links are so high-contrast, a user actually sees these links before they even begin to pay attention to specific elements. As a result, this test isn't the best gauge of whether white space affects the time it takes to complete a task.

A more realistic test might require users to add a comment to a blog post, using a button graphic (one that blends in with the page's primary color palette) as the trigger to add the comment. In this case, white space would likely have a bigger effect on the time it takes to complete the task, because a denser layout would make the button harder to find.

That said, SURL's report about the visual appeal of white space is definitely worth checking out. The full report can be found at **psychology.wichita.edu/surl/usabilitynews/2W/whitespace.htm**.

Filling in the gaps

White space is an effective alternative to using graphics to divvy up a page into clear sections because of how the human brain works to fill in gaps. When we watch a movie, the individual frames on a reel of film whiz by us at roughly 30 frames per second. Our brains fill in the rest and fool us into thinking we are seeing real, uninterrupted motion. When we look at half of a broken, ceramic mask, we "see" the whole face. Our brains fill in the gaps.

When we look at a Web page, the same thing happens.

Two elements spread far apart appear to have little or no relationship to each other, while two elements positioned more closely together appear directly related. This is why **OK** and **Cancel** buttons are often next to each other, while a **Save As** button in the same dialog box, which provides a very different function, might appear further to the left, separated from the **OK** and **Cancel** buttons.

In both of these examples, we *see the separation*. We don't need graphics to tell us there's a division between one section and another—we can see it just fine. Just like we see the close relationship of two elements positioned next to each other and the lack of meaning between two elements positioned far apart, we can see that there is a difference between *this* column and *that* column even without a vertical line to separate them.

White space does a good enough job of clearly separating areas of a page without relying on the use of graphics (which must be processed by the user's brain).

Instead of relying on graphical dividers to segregate sections of application screens, we can usually rely on white space. White space gives us the same separation between elements without the extra visual load of the graphical lines the user would need to process when glancing at the page.

White space also weighs less, in terms of file size, than graphics, so pages can load more quickly.

Cleaning up task flows

Task flows are a prime area for reduction and refinement. Unnecessarily complicated screen sequences go from mildly tedious to flat-out annoying in a very short time, especially when the task is performed regularly. Decreasing the number of screens a user must visit to complete a task improves workflow and makes application more obvious.

In the aforementioned task-management application, a simple **Create New Task** link would make the process of setting up a new project much quicker. Yes, the addition of such a link on the Task Details screen would add clutter to that page, but the cost is minimal compared to the reward of an improved workflow.

In many Web-based email applications, users have two options for how to view messages. They can either display the Inbox in one screen and open individual messages in a new window or separate page, or they can choose to show a Preview pane on the Index page and read email messages without switching to another screen or opening a new window. The latter of these two options consolidates the workflow, decreases the number of page loads, makes window management simpler (in cases where messages are displayed in a new window), and makes the Inbox screen significantly more useful.

Entire conversations display on a single page in Gmail. Please ignore the fact that I was talking to myself.

Google's Gmail, arguably, does the best job of managing the primary task flow for checking email. There is no option to show message previews on the Inbox screen—you must click through to a different screen to read a message—but each message is displayed in a *thread*. All messages from the same conversation are displayed on a single page, so users can get an at-a-glance view of the entire thread, and simply select any individual message in the thread to display it inline, according to its chronological position within the thread. If a message is the third reply in a thread of messages, it is displayed beneath the first two messages and above any messages received later on. This not only consolidates the workflow for users, but also maintains context.

Cleaning up task flows is often as simple as going through various tasks in an application and justifying everything that is encountered while trying to complete it. It can be time-consuming and tedious, but it's not complicated.

On every screen you come across in a task, write a list of everything that exists on the screen and give yourself a 60-Second Deadline (as discussed in Chapter 3). Scratch out anything you think you can get rid of, move those things to a new list, and save that list for later. Then go through the code and rip out everything you crossed off. If the page still works and the task can still be completed successfully, you're done. If not, you may have crossed off too many items.

Once this is done, write a list of the screens required to complete a task, and see if any of them can be consolidated. Can the part of the registration process where you collect a user's address information be moved into the same screen where you collect her preferred user name and password? If so, go for it.

In my task-management system, clients are listed on one screen, while projects are listed on another. If these two screens were consolidated, so that each client listing displayed underneath it a list of projects associated with that client, I could access both the Client Details and Project Details from the same place instead of drilling down.

Next, see if you can create shortcuts from one screen to another. If users commonly access two or three particular screens in the same session, provide links to all of them from each screen to make the jumps easier.

Finally, on screens where editing is allowed (or required), modify the design so the editing can be done inline instead of sending the user to an Edit screen and back to the read-only screen upon completion (known as a *round-trip* interaction). Inline editing is one of the best things about the rise of Ajax and DHTML. You can eliminate the need for entire screens in task flows, make the application simpler to understand, help maintain context for users (which contributes to a solid mental model), and make common operations more enjoyable.

The process of cleaning up task flows can be done at any point in your development process, including after the product has been released (in fact, this is a great excuse for releasing a new version, regardless of whether or not new features have been added). That said, it's far cheaper to do it before any code has been written. If code has already been written, money was spent to create the things that are now being cleaned up. It also means the tasks must now be retested to ensure nothing fails as a result of the improvements. Overhauling task flows while your application is still in its wireframe state, however, means you can fix things quickly and easily, and make major improvements when it's most cost-effective to do so.

Avoiding Interface Surgery

You may have noticed there is no Interface Surgery section in this chapter. There's a good reason for that.

Many of the topics in this book are related. This chapter applies to each of them, and each contributes to this chapter.

It's all related and it's all important. It's also all been said.

You've already seen examples of how to reduce clutter in an interface. The section about writing use cases in Chapter 2 described how to simplify an interaction. Chapter 3 was all about building only what's absolutely necessary. This reduces clutter by default. I've also talked about inline editing and inline validation, both of which add up to a faster and less cluttered task flow with fewer screens and fewer clicks. And designing screens in a consistent and uniform fashion contributes directly to a refined experience.

No need to say it all again.

▶ Practice Kaizen

Kaizen was first mentioned way back in Chapter 2 when I talked about how to write use cases, and again when I discussed wireframes, but kaizen can continue to be applied long after an application is built and released.

Although kaizen was originally developed as a management approach aimed at improving quality and reducing defects in manufacturing, the underlying philosophy is central to my approach to application design. Kaizen is about doing the work of improving things constantly, in little tiny ways that add up to gigantic results.

Kaizen can be applied to the way you write code in the programming language of your choice, design task flows, or refine the visual design of an interface.

One of the major benefits of kaizen is that it keeps you from worrying about making things perfect on the first try. To the contrary, it enables you to focus only on getting something done so you can start improving it incrementally. You can start with a grayscale HTML page if you like. As long as you keep improving things as you go, you're in good shape.

Abe Fettig, one of the developers for JotSpot Live, recently told me:

> *During development, we tried to keep the feature set of JotSpot Live very small and focused. There were a lot of interesting things we could have done, but our number one goal was to get the product released and in the hands of users. Our CEO Joe Kraus is fond of the saying "perfect is the enemy of the good." If you have a product that is good in its current state, something that works and provides a useful service to people, and you hold back from releasing it because there are more features you want to add, you're not doing yourself or your users a favor. At that point, your desire for perfection is getting in the way of something good. So, as we developed JotSpot Live, we concentrated on building a good 1.0 version, without trying to add every feature necessary to create the "perfect" version. And in retrospect, this simpler version is better than a more complex version would have been.*

Personally, I make it a habit to find something to improve at least once a week. Of course, my job is focused entirely on making things better, so this is pretty easy to do, but within that construct, I look for ways to improve my process, improve an interface I haven't looked at in a while, make meetings more productive, keep phone calls shorter, make wireframe elements reusable as templates, and anything else I can think of. Beyond that, I constantly refine interfaces and interactions in an effort to improve them in even the tiniest ways by making them more readable, more understandable, and less complicated.

Kaizen means iteration

Another major benefit of kaizen is that it enables us to get products in the hands of testers more quickly. The sooner a user starts using real screens to deal with real interactions and complete real tasks, the better. Wireframes, use cases, and mockups are great for planning a design and getting the ideas worked out, but things inevitably change once our designs go from paper to screen. It's at this point that we see how an application *really* works. Putting our designs in front of beta testers is what allows the truth about our work to come out into the light.

Abe Fettig told me:

> From there we developed JotSpot Live by doing a lot of fast iterations. I wrote the code, and Joseph Wain did the CSS and graphic design. We'd push an updated version up to our testing server every day or two. We had a group of test users that started out mostly internal and grew to include a lot of people outside the company as JotSpot Live grew more mature and we got closer to release.

There's always a way to improve an application (and no, I don't mean by adding things to it). And every time you make a small improvement to an interface, doors open up for improving the new version. But none of the changes cause any major disruption in your work, because tiny changes take almost no time at all, so you can keep plugging away at the activity of building sites and software without becoming buried in documentation and conversation about all the improvements you've made.

Kaizen means iteration. To genuinely improve our applications in the long run, we need to repeatedly go over them, see where things can be improved, make changes, and put new versions in the hands of real users to prove the changes are better. Wash, rinse, repeat.

The 5S approach

5S is another Japanese improvement process originally developed for the manufacturing industry. And just like kaizen, 5S translates well to interface design and application-development processes.

In fact, this book has discussed every aspect of 5S without ever mentioning it specifically (until now, anyway). But while the whole concept of designing the obvious can be wrapped up by these five points, it's most appropriate to describe 5S in context of the topics of reduction and refinement, because each point of the 5S system contributes directly to both topics.

The rest of this section is a summary of each piece of the 5S system and how it relates to designing the obvious.

Seiri (Sort)

Seiri is about sorting through tools and other materials to determine what must be retained and what can be thrown out or stored. In manufacturing, seiri produces a safer environment by keeping unnecessary items out of the way of workers, so they can be more steadily productive.

In Web terms, seiri can be thought of as sorting through features, interface elements, and screens to minimize an application—or a single screen—to its most essential parts.

To sort through these things properly, you have to Know What To Build, which includes knowing what *not* to build. Even after a product is developed, however, we can go through an application repeatedly in an ongoing effort clean it up and get unnecessary elements out of it.

Seiton (Straighten)

Seiton refers to arranging things into their most efficient and accessible arrangements. In other words, order should be maintained relentlessly so resources are easy to access.

In Web applications, this is about designing for uniformity so that users can derive meaning from a page's content based on how it is laid out.

Seiso (Shine)

Seiso is about keeping clean, tidy workplaces. Cleaning should be a frequent activity and should always be aimed at polishing up anything losing its shine.

On the Web, seiso can relate to improving or updating the look of graphical elements, devoting attention to more perfect alignment and distribution among page elements, and devising color palettes that contribute to the overall mood and personality of the application.

Seiketsu (Standardize)

Seiketsu is about leveraging standards to enable consistency. Online, adhering to standards means using proper semantic markup in Web pages and keeping the code used for presentation and content clearly separated.

HTML is designed to identify the structure of content. Headings are marked as headings, paragraphs as paragraphs, and so on. CSS, on the other hand, is used strictly for the presentation of the marked-up content. The standard use of these two technologies together improves the accessibility, maintainability, changeability, and sustainability of Web content. But seiketsu goes far beyond markup.

Seiketsu also means establishing a set style for an application to which all screens can conform, so each screen enables a user to maintain her mental model, and makes it easier for her to learn and orient herself to new screens.

Standardization can go a long way. Many companies maintain style guidelines that detail when and how radio buttons, checkboxes, and other elements should be used and how they should look and work. This can even be extended into a design pattern library, as discussed in Chapter 7. In this case, the library as a whole can be refined one pattern at a time and applied to multiple applications successively, so that a suite of tools can all be improved based on a single standard.

Shitsuke (Sustain)

Shitsuke is about sustaining the work of each of the elements in the 5S system for the long haul.

Improvement (kaizen) should not come in small waves and then fade away. It should be kept up on a permanent basis. The repeated process of reduction to retain only what's needed in a screen or application (seiri), the arrangement of elements into their most effective forms (seiton), the polishing of what's left (seiso), and the standardization of screens and interactions throughout multiple applications (seiketsu) are all processes that should be maintained.

The long-term effort to refine the applications we construct is how we create solutions that are effective and desirable, both now and later.

▶ Eliminate Waste

Another way to reduce and refine is not in the application itself, but rather in the *process* of creating Web applications.

Many companies step through a lengthy and complicated process each time a new application is designed and built. This process often begins with the creation of a **Vision Document**, which outlines the business goals and desires for a new application. This can be followed by a **Software Requirements Specification (SRS)**, which details the features the application must offer. And this, in turn, can be followed by a **Functional Specification**, which describes how features should behave, look, and work, complete with both high- and low-level use cases. The creation of all these documents can lead to the design of wireframes (iterated repeatedly until approved), the conversion of the wireframes into final artwork, and finally, the construction, testing, release, and marketing of the application.

Even when an application is extraordinarily simple, this process can take months. It's a highly wasteful process that often results in an application no better (and usually worse) than if the first three documents had been skipped and the developers went straight from use cases to code, with graphics created Just In Time.

In many cases, in fact, the people doing the research for a new product—product comparisons, user research, and so on—are not the same people who must create the wireframes and artwork for the application. This creates a large disconnect. The people with all the knowledge are on one side of a cubicle divider, while the designers are on the other. This disconnect means those who did the research must dump a ton of information on the designer, who must then translate the information into a design. This often results in hours of impromptu meetings between the designer and the researcher to clarify requirements and better understand what needs to be designed. Quite wasteful.

Cleaning up your process

Cleaning this whole mess up can be highly beneficial—to the company and its users. In addition to cleaning up the interface for an application, we need to clean up the process used to build them.

Specifications

First, stop relying on specifications.

It's perfectly understandable that in many companies, specifications (aka *specs*) must be written. Typically, they're required to get buy-in from management and development teams and such to build the application in the first place. Beyond this, however, they have very little effect on reality. Applications almost never adhere to them, and they're almost never updated to reflect changes made to an application's design once development has started.

Furthermore, specs are usually about a million pages long, and no one really has the time to read them. Designers want to know about the activity so they can create a design that supports it. Developers want to know how the application will function. And marketers want to know how they can market the thing. Because specs are so long (and usually extremely boring), they fail to meet any of these needs effectively.

Once the development project has been approved and is in motion, put the spec away and stop worrying about it. At this point, your goal should be to Know What To Build.

Design now, not later

I also strongly recommend turning the application designer and the researcher into a two-person team. When a knowledgeable designer is involved from the beginning, he can help decide which features are absolutely essential, study the activity the application is meant to support to gain a thorough under-standing of it, and begin creating wireframes *right away* instead of struggling through a researcher-to-designer brain-dump later on and guessing his way through the design.

The designer is the one who needs to understand the activity the most, so that he can effectively design an application that supports it. If research is to be done, the designer should be there, doing it. Sketches can be created the moment an epiphany strikes, and wireframes and use cases can be created and revised all along the way.

When the designer has *all* the information and knowledge he needs to design an effective application, the application will, indeed, become more effective.

▶ Put Just-In-Time Design and Review To Work

Sadly, many companies skip the design process completely, leaving it up to programmers to "design" software themselves, making spur-of-the-moment decisions that greatly, and often adversely, affect the experience of using the application. When design is left up to programmers, applications often become complicated, extremely difficult to use, and bloated with features that, while giving marketers a hefty list of bells and whistles to cite in mar-keting collateral, actually inhibit the ability of most users to use the software effectively to accomplish their goals.

As long as this remains true, **Just-In-Time Design** and **Just-In-Time Review** are viable and necessary alternatives.

Just-In-Time (JIT) is the process of acquiring and delivering materials right when they're needed, as opposed to maintaining a surplus. In Web terms, this translates to Just-In-Time Design, which involves doing design work right at the spur of the moment—the moment right after someone has decided to add something to the interface and right before the programmer starts producing code.

JIT Review, on the other hand, is used as a final opportunity to reduce and refine a solution once it's been built.

JIT is especially appropriate when a development team practices **Extreme Programming**, which creates a constant state of in-flux prioritization, but it can be used in any company to improve the state of an application before the latest version is released to users.

JIT Design

JIT Design generally entails holding a quick meeting before the coding starts for a new feature (or some other change to an application) to brainstorm and decide how a new piece of the software will behave, how it will be accessed or invoked, and how it will look and flow. This meeting can take five minutes or three hours, but it must be done, and it should always include someone with user-interaction know-how. If you don't have any experts around, grab the person with the most earnest level of interest in the subject and give him or her ownership (people tend to step up to even Extreme responsibility when given ownership of the result).

During a JIT Design meeting, one programmer, one designer, one user, and one whiteboard should be present. Other people can come too, but the fewer the better. More voices only make more debate. The meeting requires exactly what is needed for the purpose: a representative user (usually an internal employee) to talk about what he or she needs and wants, a designer to interpret those needs and make suggestions about possible solutions, a programmer to determine the feasibility of the suggestions and begin devising a coding plan, and a whiteboard on which to sketch interface ideas and list requirements.

A digital camera is handy, also, so you can photograph the whiteboard sketches to keep a record of the meeting and either keep the interface ideas fresh in the developer's mind or give the designer a reference point from which to create a wireframe.

To begin the meeting, simply present the problem that must be solved. Everyone should then try to justify the change to the software—it needs to be determined whether the problem is really a problem by trying to talk yourselves out of it (e.g., is there already a way for the user to do this? Is it the right solution? Does this change help 80 percent of our users?). If the change is not justifiable, the meeting is over. One of the best ways to reduce an application's complexity is to avoid adding anything new to it in the first place.

If the problem really is a problem and must be solved, attendees should brainstorm possible solutions based on the representative user's needs and desires. Everyone can contribute ideas, but the resident user-experience expert should be the one who leads the conversation. JIT Design requires fast thinking, so be sure the person leading this conversation is able to produce design ideas quickly and consistently.

The meeting should not end until everyone has a clear idea about what to build and why.

The result of such a meeting may or may not involve assigning the task of creating wireframes for the new interaction. Wireframes are preferable, but when there's no time, at least the programmers will have a good idea of what to build and how it should behave prior to making impulsive decisions that lead to a weak design.

JIT Review

The other time JIT comes into play—the time most relevant to this chapter—is when the coding has been completed, as a bookend to the Design meeting that took place prior to coding. JIT Review, as the name implies, is about reviewing what was built to make sure it adheres to what was previously agreed upon and to see how it can be improved prior to release.

In the fast-paced Web world, there is usually very little time to review, let alone *refine*, an interface before it goes out the door, especially if you don't write the code yourself. Performing a JIT Review, however, is infinitely better than doing nothing at all, so try as hard as you can to incorporate JIT Review at the end of every iteration cycle prior to release.

In most cases, a meeting is not necessary for JIT Review (though you can certainly review the solution as a group and decide collectively how to refine it). Once the proposed solution is built and is available for testing by those who developed the solution in the first place, each person involved can simply review the implementation from his or her own desk. This is true anytime—even if ample time was allowed for design work earlier in the process.

Each person should try to interact with the solution with the same goals in mind that users will have when using the final product. Go through the interaction once and make mental notes about anything that isn't completely obvious, and then go through it again with the goal of discovering ways to improve it. Make notes about how to refine the solution—how to make it better adhere to a user's mental model, take less time, and become less complicated and more error-proof.

Stick all the notes into an email or, more preferably, a bug report, and send it off to the group. When everyone has made their notes, a quick conversation is usually enough to decide how to proceed. Make the changes, test the new version, and release it to the world.

One of the best things about the Web is that it's conducive to constant change. An application doesn't have to be perfect the first time. You should certainly aim to present a good solution the first time out, but don't be afraid of imperfect solutions. The second you're done with one version, you can start iterating through the next one. Eventually, each and every part of the application will have gone through several iterations and the application will develop, almost by its own momentum, into a solid application that keeps users feeling confident and productive.

JIT as a solution

With complicated applications, JIT is the bare minimum of what can or should be done.

In simpler applications, however, JIT may be all that's really needed. An application team of only two or three people working in a room together can hold whiteboard sessions freely and often, so design decisions can be made and changed on a dime. (In fact, this can be quite fun and effective, as it creates a fast-paced environment of designing and coding that can produce amazing results in a very short time.)

Whenever possible, a resident expert on interaction or interface design (preferably a good, authoritative designer who's willing to *own* the interface) should be present, so he or she can make educated suggestions about how to make the particular piece of software more usable, more flowing and intuitive, and more likely to help users achieve their goals. In a worst-case scenario, where no interaction gurus are available, you should at least have a graphic designer in the conversation, so that a high aesthetic standard, guided by someone with a design background, can help improve the interactions. Whenever possible, though, your company should have someone on-site with a deep knowledge of how people actually use computers, so he or she can make educated suggestions about how to improve the experience, preferably before *and* after the coding process.

A user whose goals are ignored is a user who will never be a true fan of your software, and a true fan is the best thing a company can possibly acquire. If you cannot allow time for quality design work, you should, at the very minimum, allow JIT Design and Review to run interference between programmers and users. It may be the best chance you have to design, reduce, and refine an application before your company banks its future on something that doesn't meet the needs of its customer base.

9

Don't Innovate When You Can Elevate

▶ Elevate the User Experience

▶ Seek Out and Learn from Great Examples

▶ Elevate the Standards

▶ Take Out All the Good Lines

▶ Get in the Game

I used to work for a small eLearning company that designed courseware for large companies. One of the problems that we commonly faced, like most eLearning companies, is that the types of people for whom we designed content varied to incredible extremes.

Employees who handled baggage for an airline might be required by their employer to take some of the same administrative-type courses required by Human Resources staff, Sales staff, and those people that wave the electric wands over you as you pass through the security gates.

Different people learn different ways. We couldn't possibly expect all these different types of people to learn the same information the same way. When it comes to education, one size does not fit all.

Innovation

We decided to create an eLearning application that allowed non-linear education. Instead of forcing every user to go through the same set of screens in the same order, we would give users choices and direct different users through different paths of content based on their responses. Each person would get a version of a course adapted specifically to his or her particular learning style.

The innovation was a good idea. The concept worked well, it satisfied the need to address different learning styles, and the application was well received by clients.

Good for us.

The problem with innovative thinking

Later on, we ran into a problem with how users navigated our courses.

Typically, the **Next** button in an eLearning application advances a user to the next screen in the course, a screen the user has not yet seen. But we had added *history* to our application. Instead of forcing a user to start a section over again each time he wanted to go back to a particular screen, we tracked the pages he went to so that the **Back** button enabled him to traverse through the pages he had already seen, one by one, just like a browser.

A typical Next and Back button setup for an eLearning course.

The problem was that when a user began using the **Back** button to return to pages she'd already visited, the **Next** button did exactly what you'd think it would do—it advanced her through the same set of screens.

She eventually reached a point where the **Next** button advanced her past the last screen she'd already visited and began showing screens she had *not* visited. This is, after all, the purpose of the **Next** button.

So, we suddenly had a **Next** button with *two* purposes. This broke the single most basic rule about how users navigate courseware. And it was confusing users to no end.

Users needed to know when they stopped seeing *visited* screens and started seeing *new* ones, but the application did not indicate this in any way.

At the time this issue was being discovered, I was head down, fingers flying, writing code. Other people in the company, however, were meeting about the problem. Over the course of about a week, several people met several times to discuss ways to remedy the situation.

How could we make it clear to users that they had stopped going forward through the course history and had started seeing new screens? Should we show them some sort of message? That would affect the design for every course. Should we remove the ability to go backwards? That meant users would have to start over every time, or at least start a particular section over again. Should we simply explain it really well in our elaborate Help documentation? Sorry. No one reads Help documentation.

On and on the discussions went. We were innovators, after all. All we needed was some time to think it through and we'd come up with something amazing. But it just wasn't coming together.

Elevation

One day, I caught wind of the problem and suggested we create an animated button to replace the existing Next button.

When users went through the course normally, they would see the Next button, as expected. When users went backwards through screens, however, the Next button would convert into a Forward button via a simple animation. It would also change color, so users would have an extra little indication that the button now meant something new. Once a user reached the last visited screen, the button would animate again and convert back into a Next button, to indicate the next screen would be a new one.

Converting the Next button into a Forward button with a simple animation eliminated the confusion without innovative interface wizardry.

Twenty minutes later, we had a working version on a testing server. It worked extremely well. Everyone understood it immediately. The confusion was gone.

Innovation can be great thing, when it's needed, but what's needed in most cases is not innovation. It's *elevation*.

▶ Elevate the User Experience

The company I worked with spent a week trying to come up with an innovative way to let a user know when the Next button was going to take her to a screen she hadn't yet seen. But any solution that required an innovative, new interface gadget wouldn't really solve the problem, but rather complicate it—and our code—even more.

Innovations can be cool, and are often just what is needed to solve a problem. But innovations are expensive. They typically take a substantial amount of time to implement, require loads of trial-and-error experimentation, and are just as likely to fail as they are to succeed.

Besides that, most people are simply incapable of coming up with brilliant, innovative ideas *all the time*. Big ideas are few and far between. Most of the time, ideas are small.

Small enough to work.

Most of the time, companies and applications don't need big ideas. They need little ones that make small improvements *right now*.

The kaizen approach is about making frequent, incremental changes that improve things steadily and constantly.

These advances make for ongoing, positive changes that can be planned, designed, implemented, and tested very easily and quickly. They're also cost-effective, because it hardly takes any time at all to make small changes (at least, in comparison to expensive innovations), and the result often has such a high return that the investments are extremely easy to justify.

Elevation is about being more polite

One simple way to incrementally improve an application is to make it more polite.

If your application is any less polite than a really attentive and caring store clerk, iterate over the design until it becomes that polite. Your application may be the best source of customer service your company can provide. Make sure it does its job well.

What makes a polite application? Generally speaking, the absence of rudeness is all it takes. The applications that demonstrate the traits outlined in this book are more polite by default. Here are some other ways to be polite:

Don't interrupt the user's workflow. Javascript alerts, errors that could have been prevented, confirmation messages, unnecessarily complicated interactions, and confusing task flows are all things that show off an application's rude nature. Get rid of the errors. Write meaningful error messages when they are needed.

Make it easy for the user to get her job done. Pages with elements strewn all over the place without any sense of uniformity are rude because users have a harder time determining the flow of the interaction. Screens that lack visual structure are rude because users are forced to guess what's important and what isn't. Help users get up to speed quickly.

Don't force the user to understand anything that's not relevant to the job she's doing. Applications that require understanding of the underlying system to be productive are rude because they force users to bend to the whims of developers instead of relying on their own mental models. Hide the system, so that users can rely on their mental models to work with an application and be productive without heaving to learn too much. Following these rules is a giant step towards a more polite solution.

Elevation means giving your software a better personality

One of the most difficult character traits to design in an application is its personality, but a "winning" personality can be one of the best ways to elevate the user experience.

Being polite is essential to creating a good user experience, but beyond this are more subjective factors, like the *tone* of an application, that enable users to connect with our applications in a more positive way.

People connect emotionally to the things they use. If a coffeemaker is difficult to use, the user's primary connection to it is one of frustration and resentment. But if the appliance makes it easy to brew great coffee, looks nice, maintains well, and does its job consistently, users feel at ease while using it.

The coffeemaker doesn't even have to match other appliances. Usually, in fact, quirky and fun designs make items more appealing. They appeal to the user's personality, not just the user's goal for the product.

For example, Skobee (www.skobee.com)—designed to enable groups of friends to coordinate plans together around events users create—is filled with bright colors, upbeat icons, and text written in a friendly, conversational tone that tells users it's okay to have fun. The overall vibe of the application is such that it invites users to poke around and explore. Check things out. Goof off.

Skobee uses a lively and fun design style to add personality to the act of making plans.

Personality is determined largely by how things look in an application, but copy is also important. Stuffy phrases like "Update your profile to include a photograph, scheduled events, and a contact list" won't fly at Skobee. Instead, statements like "Your profile is lookin' a little shabby" and "Add a picture so everyone can see your smiling face" are shown on the Profile screen.

Using the same language they would use to talk to their own friends, Skobee developers added personality to the application that not only helps contribute to the overall product experience, but is also helpful in getting users up to speed.

No one ever said the Web had to be boring. Let's liven it up a little.

Elevation means creating "On-Demand Interfaces"

It's important to look not only at the details of an application, but also what character traits the controls represent. We need to understand not only how a drag-and-drop interaction works, but also why it's effective in the first place.

In Google Page Creator, for example, we can drag an image around within its container box, or drag it from one box to another. We can resize it by selecting it and choosing a size option from a small, image-specific toolbar that appears. We can format text by selecting it and choosing formatting options from the main toolbar. We can do all these things in many desktop applications, but they're not typical of Web applications.

Text can be formatted in Page Creator without leaving the main interface.

So what is it about these interactions that make Page Creator so easy to learn and use? Part of it is the implementation, because the design of an interaction is vital to helping users understand how it works, but it's also the character trait it represents. Page Creator is responsive. It offers what I like to call an **On-Demand Interface** (ODI), and this results in an application that is easy to understand, reacts and adapts to user input in a smooth and appealing way, and generally "just works."

An ODI offers users the features they need—where they need them and when they need them. Page Creator offers the image toolbar the moment after a user selects an image. It allows us to move an image any time we want, without taking a round-trip to an editing screen. It lets us format text without pogo-sticking in and out of popup windows designed for text formatting. We can do it all right there in the main interface, without ever leaving the page.

This is how an On-Demand Interface works.

ODIs reduce both the number of steps involved in a task and the complexity of each one. Functionality is provided when and where the user needs it, exposing features in an on-demand fashion. ODIs allow users to interact with an application in a way that facilitates productivity. They appear to adapt to the user. As a result, the user experience is improved dramatically, and user satisfaction is taken to much higher levels.

These character traits—responsiveness, speed, a streamlined mental model, and so on—are what make the application great. The implementation of the design is a huge part of its effectiveness, but only because it means the implementation effectively supports the underlying principle.

In other words, when we Know What Makes It Great and Know The Best Ways To Implement It, we can design applications that not only live up to a user's expectations, but also stand out from the crowd by providing an elevated user experience.

▶ Seek Out and Learn from Great Examples

Throughout this book, we've looked at applications like DropSend, Squidoo, and Google Page Creator, among others. These are all great applications, but this is not an exhaustive list, by any means. There are many other great applications out there, and while finding them isn't always easy, studying them is an effective way to gain more insight into how to design the obvious.

Inspiration

Studying great Web applications is also an effective way to get some inspiration.

Backpack offers us a new approach to organization for small projects. Page Creator offers us a quick way to create basic Web pages. Blinksale offers us a graceful solution to the difficult task of managing invoices to multiple clients. And Meebo offers us a way to send instant messages in a Web page.

All of the design problems these applications solve have been solved in a myriad of other ways over the years, but these simple Web applications have taken a new look at the problems and presented interesting and engaging new solutions.

We can find inspiration in existing applications, common problems (like keeping track of bookmarks on multiple computers), and even installed solutions like word processors and spreadsheet applications. These are all things that can be looked at from a new perspective and redesigned for use on the Web.

When asked how 37signals comes up with new application ideas, Jason Fried even suggests the outside world can be a good place for inspiration:

> *We're inspired by everyday simple problems. We're not interested in solving the huge problems. We're interested in solving the simple ones. Those are the ones people have to deal with every day. So it's those simple problems that inspire us to build simple tools to help people solve them. Nature is always a good place to look for really refined solutions too. There's lots of inspiration in nature. There's very little in nature that doesn't work. If it doesn't work it's been phased out a long time ago. So looking closely at the natural world really opens your eyes to wonderful and creative solutions.*

▶ Elevate the Standards

Standards are a wonderful thing, because they give us solid ground to stand on when designing applications. But for the Web to progress, we need to find ways to elevate the standards and drive the possibilities of the Web further and further.

Many designers resist standards, saying that standards leave no room for innovation. But there's definitely a middle ground here. Between standards and innovation is *elevation*.

The Web would have never reached the point it's at now without a constant push toward new solutions and technologies that give the Web more power and more sophisticated possibilities for interaction. These technologies do this by improving what's already possible. (The W3C's HTML specification hasn't changed in years, but other technologies keep pushing the limits of what it can do by working within the constraints of HTML.)

We don't need to innovate to make things better. Most often, we can elevate the standards and achieve very effective results that incrementally push the envelope.

In fact, it's especially important to *avoid* innovation when introducing new interaction styles on the Web, because users expect things to work the way they always have, and often have a difficult time learning new paradigms. It's far more effective to leverage existing paradigms and try to improve upon them in smaller, less dramatic ways.

The inline editing features of Page Creator make editing a Web page very simple, but users commonly expect to have to perform round-trip editing because they're not yet used to the notion of inline editing. This means the application now has a slight learning curve. Typically, users figure out how to use it very quickly, because its feature set and interactions are largely self-evident, but not *every* feature is as obvious as it could be.

The ability to drag an image from one side of a page to the other, for example, can be difficult if the user doesn't understand the meaning of the mouse icon that displays when an image is selected. It often takes a little time to assess the page and experiment with the tools to figure out how to move an image.

The key to making editing features like this successful is to apply some instructive design. If rolling over the image also displayed the word "drag" next to the mouse pointer, it might be much clearer to users that the mouse icon shown means the object can be dragged. This small addition can clarify the interaction and lower the learning curve. The instructive element is also insignificant enough that it won't annoy more experienced users.

That said, many users become familiar and confident with Page Creator within about 15 minutes. For an application used to design entire Web pages, this is very impressive.

For Google, the key to success was to offer elegant task flows and interactions that are easy to learn and use.

Be smart about it. If you can prove that your way is better, then you're onto something. If you can't, rely on the standards until you come up with something that *is* better.

▶ Take Out All the Good Lines

Ernest Hemingway once said, "Write the story, take out all the good lines, and see if the story still works."

It's counterintuitive, but removing the good lines from an application truly is the right way to achieve great design. The good lines are the features that are flashy and cool, that don't really contribute directly to an effective application, that exist only because of their sex appeal (as sexy as Web applications can get, anyway). The good lines are the features that the Marketing department might absolutely love, but most users will find cumbersome because they get in the way of the 20 percent of features that really matter.

When you take out all the *good* lines, what are left are the *best* lines. When there is nothing cool or sexy in the way, the features that matter are allowed to shine, and the whole user experience becomes significantly better.

When you take out everything that makes an application "competitive," what is left are the parts that make it better than the competition. What's left are the parts that let people get what they need and get out.

Elevating the user experience is not about adding features to make an application stand out from the crowd. It's about taking things away until the heart of the application is allowed to shine through. Elevation is about reduction. It's about focus. It's about kaizen.

The best software is less software.

▶ Get in the Game

Interaction designers and usability experts have a specific role to fill: to Know What To Build, Know What Makes It Great, and Know The Best Ways To Implement It.

When you work to meet these goals in the real world, you have to be able to make decisions in the interest of producing tangible results. Real applications have real design problems with real design solutions. Decisions must be made constantly in an effort to create these solutions and get things done.

Decisions are not always easy. Sometimes they're snap decisions based on very little information. Sometimes they're well-informed decisions based on long hours of usability testing and research. Whatever the case, the decisions need to be made.

Even though the most accurate answer to a design problem is usually, "It depends," the only way to move forward and get things done is to say, with great authority, *"This is how it must be done."*

When no one is willing to step up and say this, software is designed by accident, according to the whims and snap decisions of developers, managers, marketers, and anyone else who has an opinion. History has proven this is the wrong way to go. It's why we end up with so many bad applications and so few great ones.

No one really has all the answers—not even me. Every project will contain at least one design problem that lies outside the scope of this book, rendering it useless as an aid to help you make a decision right when you need it the most—when you need a little truth about the best way to design your application. But I offer you one simple fact:

Truth is a moving target.

What's true right now will very likely not be true forever. What's true for one solution will not be true for another. Design patterns will change. The capabilities of the Web will change. The way people interact with the Web will change. So you may not be able to be right 100 percent of the time, but your ability to make decisions and get things done will get you through every project. Use that.

Don't be afraid to make decisions. It will hurt you in the long run.

Next time you find yourself saying "It depends," pretend you have no options but one. When you determine, and you will, which option you are most afraid to lose, choose that one. *Make the decision.*

Final note

Almost everything about design is subjective. It's very difficult to quantify results in the field of design. The only way to really know if your design is working is to put it out there and see what happens. Great designs fail. Terrible designs succeed. Almost nothing goes as expected. But sometimes, a great design sneaks through and gets noticed.

When that happens, it's because someone was unafraid to make the tough decisions and design the obvious.

That person can be you.

I leave you with this note:

Web application designers are not screen designers, usability experts, researchers, or visionaries. They are all of these things. Great software requires great understanding. Only then can designers be in a position to say, with great authority, "This is how it must be done." And only then will they be right to do so.

Now, go forth… and design the obvious.

*   *   *   *   *   *   *   *   *   *

To continue reading my thoughts on designing the obvious, visit my site at www.rhjr.net. You can even use the contact form there to email me directly.

Index